The Power of the Resurrected Body

"Dr. Evans provides valuable understanding regarding the intersection of the body and the self—the real us. He insightfully observes Jesus' body to unlock the truth that our bodies are a facet of who we are at our core and have even greater and higher purposes central to life here and in the hereafter. A great addition to an important topic."

—**Christian L. Ramsey**, post-doctoral fellow, School of Divinity, Regent University

"In his most recent book, The Power of the Resurrected Body, George Evans states that his aim is to 'contribute to a deeper comprehension of the complex interplay between physicality, spirituality, and the divine.' His insightful study challenges traditional—sometimes understudied and problematic—dualistic notions that have taken hold in the church as to the relationship of the body and to the spiritual aspects of humanity. When our human bodies matter more, adjustments need to be made across the theological spectrum. The work we do in the world becomes even more critical in God's cosmic plan, the this-worldly aspects of salvation overtake more escapist views of 'being saved for eternity.' With the production of this work, perhaps a planned systematic theology resulting from the implications of this anthropological position is in order. I suspect we will hear more from Evans in the coming years."

—**Gary B. Agee**, lead pastor, Beechwood Church of God, Camden, Ohio

"With theological sensitivity, Evans unfolds the often-overlooked implications of Jesus' resurrected body for the life of faith. Human existence is presented as an integrated whole—at once spiritual and material—grounded in the risen body of Christ. Through this lens, the resurrection emerges as a transformative reality that informs our understanding of redemption, human identity, and eschatological hope."

—**Brent Rempel**, lecturer in theological studies, Stark College and Seminary

The Power of the Resurrected Body

Implications for Faith and Theology

GEORGE C. EVANS JR.

WIPF & STOCK · Eugene, Oregon

THE POWER OF THE RESURRECTED BODY
Implications for Faith and Theology

Copyright © 2025 George C. Evans Jr. All rights reserved. Except for brief quotations in critical publications or reviews, no part of this book may be reproduced in any manner without prior written permission from the publisher. Write: Permissions, Wipf and Stock Publishers, 199 W. 8th Ave., Suite 3, Eugene, OR 97401.

Wipf & Stock
An Imprint of Wipf and Stock Publishers
199 W. 8th Ave., Suite 3
Eugene, OR 97401

www.wipfandstock.com

PAPERBACK ISBN: 979-8-3852-0181-5
HARDCOVER ISBN: 979-8-3852-0182-2
EBOOK ISBN: 979-8-3852-0183-9

VERSION NUMBER 01/13/25

Unless otherwise indicated, all Scripture quotations are from New Revised Standard Version Bible, copyright © 1989 National Council of the Churches of Christ in the United States of America. Used by permission. All rights reserved worldwide.

Scripture quotations marked (CEV) are from the Contemporary English Version Copyright © 1991, 1992, 1995 by American Bible Society. Used by Permission.

Scripture quotations marked (ESV) are from The ESV® Bible (The Holy Bible, English Standard Version®), © 2001 by Crossway, a publishing ministry of Good News Publishers. Used by permission. All rights reserved.

Scripture quotations marked (GNT) are from the Good News Translation in Today's English Version- Second Edition Copyright © 1992 by American Bible Society. Used by Permission.

Scripture quotations marked (NIV) are from the Holy Bible, New International Version®, NIV®. Copyright © 1973, 1978, 1984, 2011 by Biblica, Inc.™ Used by permission of Zondervan. All rights reserved worldwide.

Scripture quotations marked (RSV) are from Revised Standard Version of the Bible, copyright © 1946, 1952, and 1971 National Council of the Churches of Christ in the United States of America. Used by permission. All rights reserved worldwide.

Scripture quotations marked (KJV) are taken from the King James Version and are in the public domain.

I dedicate this book to my mother, Vanzetta, who inspired in me a deep love for Jesus, a commitment to living his teachings, and a desire to explore all there is to know about him.

May the God of peace himself sanctify you entirely; and may your spirit and soul and body be kept sound and blameless at the coming of our Lord Jesus Christ. The one who calls you is faithful, and he will do this.
—1 Thess 5:23

Contents

Preface | xi
Acknowledgments | xvii
Abbreviations | xix

1 Making Flesh | 1
2 Altering Views of the Body | 23
3 Resurrecting the Body | 51
4 Locating Heaven | 72
5 An Evolution of Ideas | 84

Bibliography | 105
Index | 107

Preface

OUR SENSE OF SELF shapes the entirety of our existence, even as external influences mold various aspects of our complex being within our surroundings. The core of who we are remains unchanged. In his sermon on eternity, John Wesley discusses how every part of creation is constantly changing. He explains that this change is due to the presence of ethereal fire in all things. This fire acts as a universal solvent, breaking down even the most solid and durable materials over time. For instance, even diamonds can be turned to dust or completely burned away when exposed to extremely high temperatures, as demonstrated by Sir Francis Bacon. Wesley also mentions that "'the elements shall melt with fervent heat.' But they will be only dissolved, not destroyed; they will melt, but they will not perish. Though they lose their present form, yet not a particle of them will ever lose its existence; but every atom of them will remain, under one form or other, to all eternity."[1]

Jesus's resurrected body bears the scars of his crucifixion with equal significance to the relationships he cultivated with those who recognized him post-resurrection. His resurrection reinforces this core claim that our sense of self cannot be destroyed, only changed in form. It is certain that all who follow Jesus into the afterlife, those presently within the kingdom of God being shaped by the Holy Spirit, referred to as the born again, will experience a bodily resurrection like Jesus. For the same Spirit that raised Jesus will also raise us and bring us into the presence of God (2 Cor 4:14).

1. Wesley, "Sermon 54," para. 7.

PREFACE

The universal resurrection signifies the ultimate culmination of eschatological events, wherein the righteous embrace their eternal existence while the unrighteous face judgment, leading to the dawn of a new heaven and earth. Understanding how individuals are positioned in this newfound realm sheds light on the concept of bodily resurrection.

Throughout history, diverse beliefs have shaped perceptions of the afterlife. Ancient Jews, particularly post-Babylonian era, held onto promises of a better existence and reunion with family in the afterlife on earth, during a time when Sheol was understood as the destination for all. First-century Christian Jews anticipated the fulfillment of promises regarding the restoration of Israel's kingdom by the Messiah, envisioning a renewed heaven and earth. Hellenist Christians, influenced by Greek notions of the immortal soul, looked forward to residing in a heavenly realm. Post-Enlightenment Christians, on the other hand, anticipate inhabiting a new heaven and earth.

Exploring these perspectives is significant not only for understanding the diverse spatial landscapes of the afterlife but also for comprehending the varying perceptions of the resurrected body within these realms. At the core of this research lies the mystery surrounding Jesus's physical existence, from his virgin birth to the empty tomb, a conundrum that has persisted unresolved in the minds of believers and nonbelievers alike. Over centuries, many Christians have viewed Jesus as both divine and human, yet only a minority have attempted to reconcile the teachings of Hellenistic Judaism with those of traditional Judaism. These teachings, potentially embodying a dualistic perspective, have not gained widespread acceptance.

Paul's expansion upon the traditional Jewish concept of the body, understood as *flesh* encompassing the entirety of a person, emerged within the cultural context of Hellenistic Judaism. This ideology sparked interest among early Jewish communities. However, within the Gospels, the Judeo-Christian tradition shifts toward encountering life as a being transformed through Christ.

PREFACE

By comparing Judaic, Greek, and Rabbinic philosophies, we uncover more than three aspects of *flesh* that align with the concept of a unified physical entity, depicted as a spatial being, and the subject of bodily resurrection.

In the introduction, "Making Flesh," Jesus fashioned a body that was both spiritual and physical, existing as a cohesive whole. At the end of life, Jesus's body, present within the tomb, unveils the truth of the body's reality.

Chapter 2 delves into significant developments in the concept of the body from the Second Temple period to the Middle Ages, as evidenced in Judaic, Greek, and Rabbinic literature. In the early church, the diverse philosophical ideas surrounding the body reached a climax when Jews and Christians diverged following the Nicene Creed (325 CE), which declared Jesus to be both divine and human in one body. This declaration marked a shift in views of Jesus's body and provided a definitive form of it. The human body is designed to bridge two realms: on earth, it is a spiritual and natural body, and in heaven, the spiritual body germinates from a natural body. While scholars have yet to offer a new concept of the body beyond being an encasement for the mind and soul, this book proposes an alternative perspective.[2] Here, the body is seen as mirroring God's spatial existence, consisting of moving parts that reflect the human's whole being.

Chapter 3 focuses on body rhetoric. The rhetoric used in the New Testament often employs literary devices that create body metaphors that are traditionally accepted as literal truths. This book aims to explore these narratives by limiting contextual meanings, in order to extract the truth where the body is inaccurately represented across cultural boundaries.

Chapter 4 views the properties of the body. The Christian concept of the new body as a whole being composed of various properties in a state of flux sheds light on the mystery of Jesus's birth, death, and resurrection. This idea offers a concept of the human image that reflects God's spatial existence, disentangling the

---

2. Kleinig, *Wonderfully Made*.

enigma surrounding these events. This research takes a stance on this issue, viewing the body as only one aspect of a whole being.

Chapter 5 not only contemplates the resurrected body in heaven but also its manifestation on earth. The Jewish belief in the literal descent of the body to Sheol provides insight into the ascent of the resurrected body to earth. In her book *Divine Bodies*, Candida Moss argues that the body must be preserved in its entirety or at least enough of it must be preserved for the resurrected *me* to remain the same as the *me* that exists now.[3] This exploration delves into the significance of the resurrected body on earth, contrasting viewpoints on body preservation and its role in the afterlife. The study advocates for the preservation of the body for continuity, proposing that Jesus's pre-resurrection body already foreshadowed his post-celestial form and was thus prepared for the afterlife. The promise of bodily resurrection for believers parallels Jesus's own resurrection, as all who follow him are destined for a similar fate.

By examining various historical and cultural perspectives, the study clarifies the evolution of beliefs about the afterlife. It traces the shift from ancient Jewish expectations of an earthly paradise to Hellenistic and post-Enlightenment Christian visions of heavenly realms. These diverse perspectives influence our understanding of the resurrected body and its spatial context.

The mystery surrounding Jesus's physical existence, from birth to the empty tomb, remains a focal point of inquiry. While various theological interpretations have emerged over centuries, the tension between Jesus's divinity and humanity persists. Paul's theological elaborations within the context of Hellenistic Judaism offer insights into the concept of the body as encompassing the entirety of a person, influencing early Jewish communities. However, the emphasis within Judeo-Christian tradition shifted toward viewing humanity as transformed beings in light of the Gospel narratives.

In examining the significance of the resurrected body on earth, the study engages with differing viewpoints on body preservation and continuity. Candida Moss's argument for the preservation of

---

3. Moss, *Divine Bodies*.

PREFACE

the body underscores the importance of continuity between one's pre- and post-resurrection existence. This perspective suggests that Jesus's pre-resurrection body already anticipated his celestial form, offering insight into the nature of the resurrected body and its preparation for the afterlife.

Acknowledgments

THIS BOOK WOULD NOT have been possible without the love and support of my wife, Sandra. I will always be grateful for having you in my life.

I also give glory to God and express my gratitude to the many individuals who have contributed to my research and writing. This project has been a long journey, and I am grateful for the encouragement and assistance I have received along the way.

Abbreviations

1 En.	1 Enoch
2 Bar.	2 Baruch
HTR	*Harvard Theological Review*
Jos. *Ant.*	Josephus, *Jewish Antiquities*
JTSA	*Journal of Theology for Southern Africa*
J.W.	*Jewish War*, Josephus
NovT	*Novum Testamentum*
OTP	*The Old Testament Pseudepigrapha*. Edited by James H. Charlesworth. 2 vols. New York: Doubleday, 1983, 1985
Plato, *Resp.*	Plato, *Respublica* (*Republic*)
Pss. Sol.	Psalms of Solomon
Sib. Or.	Sibylline Oracles
SJT	*Scottish Journal of Theology*
WBC	Word Biblical Commentary
ZNW	*Zeitschrift für die neutestamentliche Wissenschaft und die Kunde der alteren Kirche*

1

Making Flesh

INTRODUCTION

THE DEBATE SURROUNDING JESUS'S resurrection draws parallels with the contentious narrative depicted in Samuel Coleridge's poem, *Rime of the Ancient Mariner*. In this tale, the crew blames the mariner for shooting a friendly seabird believed to symbolize good fortune. Consequently, they hang the bird around the mariner's neck, turning it into an emblem of guilt. Similarly, the crucifixion of Jesus, symbolically worn by Christians, serves as a poignant reminder of his sacrifice and love, but it too can appear to be a symbol of guilt.

While some see the cross as a sign of death, for Christians, it signifies Jesus's resurrection. It is true that we could spend our lives recounting our sins, but we also share how Jesus, through the cross, not only rescued us in death but also through his resurrection. Yet, this final part of the narrative can become burdensome and challenging to confront. Just as the albatross symbolizes shame in Coleridge's poem, the body of Jesus has become a source of scandal for many, and the controversies surrounding his resurrected appearance should not be underestimated.

For those who reject the notion of Jesus's divinity, and particularly deny his resurrection, Jesus is perceived as a threat. To many, he is regarded as a man, a revered prophet, and a symbol of love, but not as God. Both Jewish and Greek reactions to the narrative of Jesus can be viewed as efforts to challenge the authenticity of his existence.

The *Toledot Yeshu*, a medieval text, presents an alternative and controversial perspective on Jesus's life, challenging his divinity and offering a satirical account. It accuses Jesus of an illegitimate birth, theft of God's unspeakable name, engagement in heretical acts, and a dishonorable death. Though this text does not represent mainstream Jewish beliefs, it sheds light on the resistance to Jesus and Christianity in late antiquity.

Another challenge to the biblical narrative comes from Celsus, a second-century pagan thinker. Celsus argued that Jesus was born from an affair between Mary and a Roman soldier named Panthera. He also claimed that Christians created the Jesus story, drawing heavily on Greek myths but refusing to acknowledge it as a fable. At the core of Celsus's critique is his rejection of Jesus's divinity and the concept of resurrection. Responding to Celsus in the third century, the church father Origen refuted these claims, defending the biblical account of Jesus's miraculous conception and resurrection.

However, the real theological scandal is not just in the rejection of Jesus's divinity by certain groups, nor in claims that his body was stolen from the tomb. The deeper scandal lies in the profound mystery of Jesus's bodily resurrection, an event that defies the natural order and transcends conventional understanding of physical existence. While the gospel message may offend some and appear foolish to others, it is central to Christian belief that Jesus was conceived under the shadow of the Holy Spirit and resurrected, body included.

The resurrection of Jesus is not merely about an empty tomb but serves as a model for all believers. His visible, resurrected body after death indicates that Christian human beings will experience a similar transformation. Through spiritual rebirth, believers undergo a renewal of both body and spirit, a regeneration that mirrors Jesus's triumph over mortality.

This interpretation aligns with Christian theology, which views the resurrection as a pivotal event symbolizing victory over death and the promise of eternal life. The resurrected body represents a new, glorified existence beyond the limitations of the old, physical life.

Although certain mysteries remain, particularly regarding the incarnation (John 1:14) and the specific nature of Jesus's birth, the resurrection offers a glimpse into the transformation of human beings. Jesus's resurrected body reflects a unique existence that combines both divine and human nature. In this view, the physical body is not something to be discarded but is central to spiritual life and future resurrection.

In understanding Jesus's bodily resurrection, we recognize that the body is more than just a vessel for the spirit. It is an integral part of the human experience, created in the image of God and designed for both spiritual and physical realms. Jesus's postresurrection body illustrates that the physical and spiritual aspects of existence are not separate but intertwined, and this union will be perfected in the new creation. His resurrection provides a model of what it means to be fully restored in both body and spirit.

INCARNATION

Let us first address the myth that Jesus's flesh, formed under the shadow of the Holy Spirit, was sinful. Sin is prohibited wherever the Holy Spirit's functional role as the presence of God exists. The sacred and profane do not mix in spaces on earth or in the cosmos. In other words, Christ did not become a sinner. The phrase "who knew no sin" in 2 Cor 5:21 is a Hebraic expression that means "to have no personal experience with sin." Paul is stating that Jesus did not sin; he "was without sin" (GNT). In some languages, a verbal form is used such as "Christ never sinned" (CEV).[1] Ernst Käsemann argues that the word *sin* (ἁμαρτία) used in this context refers to punishment for sin, rather than sin as a power, which

---

1. Omanson and Ellington, *Handbook on Paul's Second Letter*.

is the usual Pauline use.² This interpretation is supported by the notion of *imparted* righteousness at the end of the verse. However, the meaning of the phrase "God appointed [ἐποίησεν] him [to be] sin" is still up for debate. Our conclusion is that the text in question is leaning on an Old Testament testimony, specifically Isa 53:10, where "offering for sin" (חטאת, ḥaṭṭā't, אשם, 'āšām) is what is implied by the word *sin* (ἁμαρτία).³ This signals the beginning of illusions about the nature of Christ's body. If Jesus had no sin, it raises the question of how he could be both divine and human.

It wasn't until 318 CE that the question of how Jesus could be both divine and human was addressed. At that time, Emperor Constantine called a council of bishops together to settle the dispute among church bishops and priests. The council concluded that the teachings of an Alexandrian priest named Arius were heretical. Arius believed that God the Father was a monad, without equal, and the creator of the only begotten son, Jesus Christ, who was created and founded before the ages, and was not of the same substance as the Father. However, the council established that Christ was of the same essence as the Father, a hypostasis, which refers to a common ousia (nature) and is used to demonstrate a likeness in substance:

> And in one Lord Jesus Christ, the only-begotten Son of God, begotten of the Father before all worlds; God of God, Light of Light, very God of very God; begotten, not made, being of one substance with the Father, by whom all things were made. Who, for us men and for our salvation, came down from heaven, and was incarnate by the Holy Spirit of the virgin Mary, and was made man; and was crucified also for us under Pontius Pilate; He suffered and was buried; and the third day He rose again, according to the Scriptures; and ascended into heaven, and sits on the right hand of the Father; and He shall come again, with glory, to judge the quick and the dead; whose kingdom shall have no end.⁴

2. Käsemann is quoted in Robinson, *Future of Our Religious Past*, 53.
3. Martin, *2 Corinthians*, 317.
4. Schaff, *History of Creeds*, 24.

While the Nicene Council addressed the essence of Christ, it did not fully explain crucial questions about Jesus's nature. As a result, the Council of Chalcedon in 451 CE was convened to resolve the ongoing dispute about the nature of Christ. The council concluded that Christ was both divine and human, the incarnation of God. This, the Fourth General Council of the church, defined that Christ remained perfect in divinity and perfect in humanity after the incarnation. Christ was consubstantial with the Father according to his divinity, and consubstantial with us according to his humanity. He was one and the same Christ, the Son, the Lord, the only begotten, to be acknowledged in two natures that were not intermingled, changed, divisible, or separable.[5] This attempt to explain the nature of Christ's humanity only solidified the mysterium, becoming a binding dogma for Christian faith. The Western church and most of the Eastern church resolved their theological differences over Christ's nature.

Although the creed was widely accepted by Christians across the world, it was not embraced by some communities in the Middle East, including the Assyrian Church of the East and the Oriental Orthodox Churches, as well as many Christians in the Persian empire. Additionally, hagiographic texts, such as biographies that excessively praise a person, often have a didactic and rhetorical tone. They are also of immense interest for understanding how Arabs and other outsiders adopted Christianity.[6] In this context, we see how hagiographic literature works in favor of Christianity, but here, it is only used as a polemic against the Caledonian creed.

This study aims to compare the literary and historical texts utilized to comprehend the beliefs of Jews and Christians. However, it is important to note that the scope of this study does not restrict our knowledge to other sources that contributed to their understanding of the human constitution. It is important to consider that the context of both first-century Christians and Jews involved a variety of influences including Greek, Roman, pagan, and Persian influences. The New Testament is similar to a modern

---

5. Bridge, "Homoousion." See also Denzinger, *Compendium of Creeds*, 148.
6. Fisher, *Rome, Persia, and Arabia*, 11.

concept of intersectionality, wherein the nature of an individual or group is interconnected through social groups and their religion. In this study, we interpret different texts not solely based on a hermeneutic approach, wherein the meaning of an action is considered the most basic fact of social life. Instead, our interpretation of the text is based on the social strands of the speaker's background woven into the oral and written text. This approach considers the cultural and historical context surrounding the text to better understand its meaning.

Transitioning from the enigma surrounding the nature of Jesus to a resolution can be initiated by examining Luke's narrative of Jesus's birth and John's Gospel account of the eternal existence of the Word. In Luke's account, Mary is overshadowed by the Holy Spirit, the giver of life, while in John's Gospel, the Word (Logos) is revealed as becoming flesh. Luke portrays the birth of Jesus from a bystander's perspective, whereas John's Gospel presents a revelation from an outward-looking perspective. To uncover the mystery of the making of the Son of Man, we must peel away the layers of malicious gossip and admit that the conception of a child by a relatively young virgin girl named Mary, who was engaged to be married to a man named Joseph, was not a moral disgrace but divine Providence. The key to understanding the nature of Jesus's birth, when the Word became flesh, begins with the acknowledgment that Jesus uncovers at least two parts of the human composition in his birth: spirit and body (John 1:14). As a consequence, the physical and spiritual body share an intimate connection that is inseparable. Christ is said to have two natures, each retaining its own properties, united in one substance. This declaration affirms that in Christ, the two natures, each retaining its own properties, are united in subsistence and one person.[7]

The birth and resurrection of Jesus can be seen as providing insight into the nature of human beings. This is evident in the characteristics of Jesus as both the Son of God and the Son of Man, with each substance possessing distinct properties. The term *Word* exclusively refers to *God*, while the term *flesh* exclusively refers to

7. Denzinger, *Compendium of Creeds*, 148.

human being. Therefore, the incarnation of Jesus should not be viewed as mere hearsay or anecdote.[8]

Tertullian of Carthage, who lived in a Roman province of Africa, taught that the Word was conjoined with the body and became one person. In Tertullian's polemic against Praxeas, he argues that Christ's being is composed of two substances: one divine and immortal and the other human. Therefore, Christ suffers as humans do. The Word is not transformed, but rather it put on flesh. Understood in this way, the body is a property of *flesh*, which refers to a human's whole being. The properties of the flesh are fashioned within, and the body of Jesus is transformed without.

Considering that the body encompasses numerous attributes, it is reasonable to suggest that the Word became flesh, a different aspect of the same entity, and united as one person. However, there are additional qualities to be explored, starting with Jesus's body and beliefs. Regrettably, the focus on the scandal has prevented us from delving into the attributes of the flesh. The Greco-Roman and Jewish cultures that were present during the life and death of Jesus provide the backdrop for comprehending the biblical texts concerning his body. However, it can be challenging to differentiate between the Jewish and Greek ideologies that intersect in Christian doctrine. Once the holy Scriptures are verbalized by speakers, the two beliefs—Jewish and Christian—appear indistinguishable in an environment influenced by Greco-Roman, pagan, and Christian ideologies.

According to Michal Bar-Asher Siegal, talmudic debates should not be considered as historical discussions that reflect Jewish-Christian dialogue about the verses in question.[9] Nonetheless, the creation of the text can still be regarded as historical as it represents genuine debates and discussions about the biblical verses. While Johann Maier found no evidence of the historical Jesus in the Talmud, he admits that the references to Jesus could have been a reaction to Christian provocation in a larger

---

8. Norris, *Christological Controversy*, 48.
9. Siegal, *Jewish-Christian Dialogues*, 22.

discussion of Christianity, in which the references were added later.[10] Peter Schäfer determined that the references to Jesus in the Talmud (third and fourth century) were satirical references to the New Testament. In addition, Theosophist George Robert Stow Mead, when researching Christian origins through the study of Talmud Jesus stories, comments:

> How few Christians to-day know anything of this subject; how few have the remotest conception of the traditions of Jewry concerning the founder of their faith! For so many centuries have they regarded Jesus as God, and everything concerning Him, as set apart in the history of the world, as unique and miraculous, that to find Him treated of as a simple man, and that too as one who misled the children of His people, appears to the believer as the rankest blasphemy. . . . Astonishing, therefore, as it appears, though Jew and Christian use the same scripture in common, with regard to their fundamental beliefs they stand over and against each other in widest opposition.[11]

The main focus of this study is to provide context for the teachings of Judaism and Greece concerning the properties of flesh. In regards to Jewish sources, it is essential to consider cross-cultural contextualization. As Michal Bar-Asher Siegal suggests, we should not be deceived by the illusion of passive observance, and we must exercise caution when comparing two sets of texts to ensure the accuracy of our conclusions.[12]

Kimberlé Crenshaw introduced the concept of *intersectionality*, which refers to the interconnected nature of social categorizations such as race, class, and gender, creating interdependent systems of discrimination or disadvantage. This concept of intersectionality, while often applied to modern social issues, can also help us understand the early Christian movement. Early Christianity did not emerge in a vacuum but was shaped by overlapping

---

10. See the survey in Maier, *Jesus von Nazareth*, 18–41.
11. Mead, *Did Jesus Live 100 B.C.?*, 5–6.
12. Siegal, *Early Christian Monastic Literature*, 12.

social, cultural, and religious influences. To fully grasp the complexities of early Christian identity, we must recognize the interplay of various social groups, cultural contexts, and religious practices that shaped its development.

In his book *The Jewish Gospels*, Daniel Boyarin argues that the division between Jews who accepted Jesus and those who did not was not as stark as often portrayed. He asserts that in the early church, there was no clear distinction between Judaism and Christianity—this division only became solidified with the development of the Nicene Creed. Initially, Jews who accepted Jesus as divine continued to see themselves as part of the broader Jewish tradition. It was only later that some began to refer to themselves as Christians. Boyarin's argument challenges the simplistic view of a sharp break between the two traditions.

Peter Schäfer builds upon Boyarin's work, noting that early Jewish and Christian identities were fluid and not defined by rigid boundaries. He observes that categories such as Jew, pagan, Christian, and even gnostic had permeable borders in the early centuries of the Common Era.[13] Within this fluidity, various groups, including Jewish Christians, gentile Christians, God-fearers, and Hellenized Jews, competed to define their identities and religious practices. These competing influences shaped the development of early Christian doctrine and practice, illustrating that early Christianity was a complex, multi-faceted movement rather than a monolithic entity.

When we examine the Gospels in this context, they reveal not only theological diversity but also their attachment to different strands of Judaism. The Gospel of Matthew, for instance, reflects a form of Judaism that was focused on maintaining Jewish law and tradition, while the Gospel of John represents a different stream, emphasizing the divinity of Christ in ways that would have resonated with Hellenized Jews and gentiles.[14] Reading the Gospels in light of other Jewish texts from the same period highlights the

---

13. Schäfer, *Jewish Jesus*, 3.
14. Boyarin, *Jewish Gospels*, 22.

complex interrelationship between early Christian thought and first-century Judaism.

A deeper exploration of early Christian and Jewish literature reveals how these texts intersect and engage with broader cultural and philosophical traditions. For instance, certain New Testament passages cannot be fully understood without considering Greek literature, hagiography from the Middle East and Persia, and rabbinic literature from the Greco-Roman world. These intersections are crucial for understanding how early Christians and Jews conceived of the human body, the soul, and their relationship to the divine.

In both Jewish and early Christian thought, the concept of the whole person was central. For Orthodox Jews, the human being was seen as a unified whole, while early Christians often distinguished between body, soul, and spirit. Rabbinic interpretations of ancient Jewish teachings, including those found in the Mishnah and the Talmud, sometimes described as many as nine different aspects of the human being. These interpretations provide valuable insights into how Jewish thinkers understood the body and soul, which in turn can illuminate early Christian views on these topics.

The virgin birth of Jesus offers a particular point of comparison between Jewish and Christian thought. While rabbinic tradition may not agree with the Christian understanding of the virgin birth, exploring these ideas within the context of rabbinic teachings can deepen our understanding of how early Christians conceptualized the incarnation. The mystery of Jesus's birth, death, and resurrection introduces a new mode of existence for believers, one that unites the material and spiritual aspects of the human being in ways that both reflect and transcend earlier Jewish thought.

VIRGIN CONCEPTION

John's Gospel is not the first mention of a virgin birth conception. While contemporary rabbinic teaching does not link the virgin conception of Jesus to Paul's allegory in Galatians, it does argue that Isaac's birth was also a virgin conception. According to the biblical story, Isaac was conceived by the barren Sarah only after a heavenly promise was made to Abraham and Sarah (Gen 18). Paul used the verse from Isaiah to support his reading that Sarah conceived Isaac through the spirit, in contrast with Ishmael's birth by the flesh. Michal Bar-Asher Siegal offers a linguistic interpretation of Paul's reading of the verses in Isa 54:1. She suggests that the antonym for הרקע, which is "barren woman," is הלותב, which is "virgin," declaring that Sarah did not have sexual intercourse (according to the Late Hebrew).[15] In Galatians Paul suggests that while one of Abraham's sons was conceived through sexual intercourse, the other was conceived in a nonsexual manner, through the spirit.

> For it is written that Abraham had two sons, one by a slave woman and one by a free woman. But the son of the slave was born according to the flesh, while the son of the free woman was born through promise. Now this may be interpreted allegorically: these women are two covenants. One is from Mount Sinai, bearing children for slavery; she is Hagar. Now Hagar is Mount Sinai in Arabia; she corresponds to the present Jerusalem, for she is in slavery with her children. But the Jerusalem above is free, and she is our mother. For it is written,
>
> "Rejoice, O barren one who does not bear; break forth and cry aloud, you who are not in labor! For the children of the desolate one will be more than those of the one who has a husband." (Isa 54:1)
>
> Now you, brothers, like Isaac, are children of promise. But just as at that time he who was born according to the flesh persecuted him who was born according to the Spirit, so also it is now. But what does the Scripture say? "Cast out the slave woman and her son, for the son of the slave woman shall not inherit with the son of the free woman." So, brothers, we are not children of the slave but of the free woman. (Gal 4:23–32)

---

15. Siegal, *Jewish-Christian Dialogues*, 111–21.

Siegal clarifies that modern scholars do not interpret Paul's writings as a reference to the notion of virgin birth because there is no connection between his story of a virginal conception and that of Jesus. However, it does appear that Paul is alluding to a proverbial body birthed by the promise as a conceptual counterpart to the physical body. While the Hebrew Bible distinguishes between spirit and flesh, it does not embrace the kind of dualism of body and soul that is characteristic of Greek thought. In the Hebrew Bible, terms referring to the soul usually denote an activity or characteristic of the body, or the entire living being, rather than a separate entity or substance.

To emphasize this point, in the theophanic experience of Abraham, God appears in human form. In Jewish writing, it is assumed that the physical body exists when reading about Abraham's engagement with God. The Hebrew Bible does not question the existence of a body when God appears; either the whole person is present, or there is no person at all. Man, as a living being, was perceived as a whole, and none of the properties of his being were separate.

Biblical scholar Robert Gundry notes that there is a pervasive understanding of Old Testament anthropology that views the body and soul as not being in contrast. Instead, man is seen as an animated body rather than an incarnated soul. However, despite this view, Gundry remains one of the most articulate proponents of a dualistic interpretation of the New Testament, as seen in his work.[16] Unfortunately, the framers and defenders of Christian creeds throughout history have almost universally affirmed or presupposed the view that the soul is distinct from the body. This view is often referred to as dualism or substance dualism because it recognizes two distinct entities that contribute to the existence of an individual human object: souls and bodies.[17] The doctrine of a disembodied intermediate state between physical death and physical resurrection is central to at least two branches of Christianity—Eastern Orthodoxy and Roman Catholicism—and is

---

16. See Murphy, *Bodies and Souls*, 146.
17. Farris, "Souls and Bodies."

commonly endorsed among others, such as Protestantism. Many have interpreted this teaching as suggesting a possible separation of the person (as a soul or spirit) from their body.[18]

I propose that we contemplate the physical embodiment of human beings, acknowledging that the body and soul are inseparable. The body is not merely a vessel for the soul, but rather a fundamental aspect of our being. We can consider both the properties of the body and the soul. Through an examination of New Testament texts that explore the mystery of Jesus's body at birth and death, we can come to understand the body as an eternal organ.

In Genesis, having sinned, Adam and Eve are forbidden access to the tree of life, cutting off the body as a developing eternal organ. However, in Jesus's birth and resurrection, the whole being is renewed based on John's Gospel. The virgin birth at the opening and the empty tomb at the close of Jesus's life bear witness that Jesus was making flesh, reconstructing man's whole being.

Nevertheless, the physical body is a dual illusion adapted for both the material and spiritual world, with each developing simultaneously, yet hidden from the other in its environment. Physical bodies in the material world change as people develop and evolve. The physical body is always in a state of flux, constantly reflecting the changes in properties within and outside of it, including the spatial world of the unseen. Karl Barth's revelation comes close to explaining the mystery of life marked by the virgin birth and the empty tomb. While his revelation is founded on the idea that humans are composed of distinct parts, he emphasizes that the *conceptus de Spiritu sancto, natus ex Maria virgine* (the conception of the Holy Spirit, born of the virgin Mary) is an event that defies explanation and must be regarded as a mystery of God's action.[19] Barth utilizes the story of the virgin birth and the empty tomb to argue for the necessity of church dogma. He cites the second clause as the starting point, which asserts that the person of Jesus Christ is the true son of a real mother, born of the body, flesh and blood of his mother, with both of them being as real as all other sons

---

18. Farris, "Souls and Bodies."
19. Barth, *Doctrine*, 181.

born of other mothers.[20] Barth would probably concur that God has the ability to reveal the nature of Jesus's body as needed. In our present time, it is increasingly vital to grasp the importance of Jesus's physical body.

Undoubtedly, moving forward requires a response similar to Peter's when he was asked by Jesus, "Who do people say that the Son of Man is?" His response was, "You are the Christ, the Son of the living God." Jesus replied, "Flesh and blood did not reveal this to you, but my Father in heaven" (Matt 16:17 ESV). To summarize, we must rely on the work of the Spirit to explain the hidden properties of human nature by examining the making of flesh. This involves appealing to two types of human experience: (1) the understanding that we are more than just our bodies, and (2) the experience of various sensations in a unified way. This way of understanding human creation leads to further questions regarding Christ's incarnation.[21] By identifying the properties of the whole being of humans, which are perceived as a collection of properties in a single spatial region without separating its parts, we arrive at a new way of understanding Christ's body and the whole being of humanity.

SPATIAL BODIES

In contemporary thought, the relationship between our physical presence and mental or spiritual presence is complex. While our bodies occupy physical space, our mental and spiritual presence can be detached, existing beyond mere physical boundaries. Our physical presence does not always guarantee our full, conscious participation in a moment or place. We experience this disconnection between the physical and the spiritual aspects of existence, recognizing that while our bodies are limited by space, our minds and spirits are not.

---

20. Barth, *Doctrine*, 185.
21. Evans, *Holy Spirit as Space*, 122.

This concept of *space* extends beyond the physical. In philosophy, *place* refers to the physical location of our bodies, while *space* can be seen as the environment occupied by different aspects of our being—mental, social, and spiritual. For someone to be fully present, these distinct aspects of existence must converge. Yet, our understanding of the physical has historically been limited to the material plane, neglecting other dimensions of being. The challenge is how to reconcile these facets of human existence, especially in light of Christian theology, where the resurrection of Jesus introduces a new mode of being that transcends the limitations of the physical body.

Through the mystery of Jesus's birth, death, and resurrection, believers receive a new mode of existence that includes a transformed body, one that operates both in the spiritual and material worlds. This new body is not confined by the physical limitations of the old. Jesus, as the incarnate Son of Man, exemplifies this union of body and spirit. His resurrection offers a model of what happens when the physical body is transformed into something new—a body that can inhabit both spiritual and material realms.

In this transformed state, the regenerated believer can experience space differently, moving beyond the limitations of the old flesh. The resurrection body, as seen in Jesus, points to a future reality for all believers—a body that no longer succumbs to death or decay but is capable of existing fully in both the spiritual and physical realms. The resurrection is not merely about reclaiming life after death; it is about embodying a new way of being, where the boundaries between the material and spiritual are transcended.

This duality of body and spirit that Jesus presents challenges our traditional notions of presence and being. While the material world confines our physical bodies, the resurrection, like Jesus, allows humans to experience the fullness of life in both the spiritual and material dimensions. This understanding reshapes our view of existence, emphasizing the interconnectedness of body, mind, and spirit in a holistic way.

Thus, the resurrection does more than offer hope of life after death—it provides a new framework for understanding human existence. The resurrected body represents the ultimate unity of the spiritual and the material, reflecting the divine intention for all creation. Jesus's resurrection invites believers to imagine a new kind of life, one that transcends the physical limitations of our current reality and points to newly created beings in new bodies that inhabit realms that transcend the constraints of their predecessors, who were unable to sustain the divine reality that Adam and Eve encountered in the garden, where they occupied sacred space.

Ever since, throughout history, humans have physically migrated from one sacred space to another, with the holiness of a place being defined by the presence of God. However, the new mode of existence believers enter after being born again transcends the constraints of physical space. This allows for a more profound experience of the divine that goes beyond traditional sacred locations. In this transformed state, the believer's existence within the mixed space of the Spirit transcends human boundaries while still engaging with physical reality. Thus, spiritual encounters with the divine occur within physical space, but are no longer confined by it. This new existence makes possible a deeper and more profound engagement with God, unrestricted by physical limitations.

Some perspectives suggest that the body and soul, mind and spirit, form a unified whole, rather than being separate entities. These views acknowledge that our physical and spiritual selves evolve together, challenging traditional dualistic notions that separate the two. Nancey Murphy's philosophy of physicalism, for example, proposes that humans are *spirited bodies*—intelligent, moral, and spiritual beings capable of communicating with God. According to Murphy, these spirited bodies are resurrected, challenging the traditional belief in an immortal soul that exists apart from the body. While I do not fully support Murphy's view, I appreciate her willingness to challenge the concept of dualism, along with those of her mentors. Her work underscores the central role the physical body plays in our spiritual experience, raising important questions about the nature of the afterlife.[22]

---

22. Murphy, *Bodies and Souls*, 22.

The postresurrection accounts of Jesus support the idea that the body and soul are interconnected. Jesus's bodily form was recognizable, suggesting that even after resurrection, he maintained his physical identity and personality. This challenges the traditional dualistic view that separates the body and soul, instead pointing to an integrated existence. Jesus's postresurrection body exemplifies the continuation of both physical and spiritual life, which evolved together in the context of the incarnation. This view significantly impacts our understanding of the afterlife, moving away from the notion of a disembodied soul and emphasizing the resurrection of the body as central to salvation.

This understanding of bodily resurrection aligns with the Old Testament emphasis on the wholeness of salvation. Rather than focusing on an immortal soul, the Old Testament points to the centrality of the resurrection of the body, as seen in passages like 2 Pet 3:13 and Rev 21:1,[23] which describe the renewal of heaven and earth. Our glorified existence finds its home in this new creation, affirming that salvation encompasses both physical and spiritual renewal, not just an escape from the body.

The human body was designed to bridge two realms: the eternal, invisible realm of God and the visible, temporal realm of creation. Created in God's image, human bodies are meant to be holy, reflecting the holiness of God himself. Therefore, the body does not solely belong to the physical world, but also to the eternal world of God. The body that Jesus possessed after his resurrection operated in both the spiritual and material realms. This suggests that the human body, in its glorified state, is suited for both the visible and invisible worlds, transcending the limitations of time and space. Jesus's resurrection body offers a glimpse into the nature of human existence—an integrated whole, where body and spirit are united, capable of engaging with both the physical and divine realms. As humans, we are designed to exist as whole beings, not as a body without a spirit or a spirit without a body.

Therefore, the whole person is the object of all God's acts, from the bestowal of dominion over the earth to the resurrection

---

23. Plantinga, *Materialism and Christian Belief*, 369.

of the dead and the end of the world. Nobody acts with just one part of themselves, but rather, each aspect of our being is interconnected and influences the others. According to A. F. C. Vilmar, when we think, we do so with our entire being, including the body, soul, and spirit. To fully appreciate the complexity and mystery of the human body, we must recognize that it is a gift, intricately designed and given to us by a higher power.[24] The body of Jesus is significant because it reveals the mystery of our personal identity and the composition of the body. The body serves to locate us in time and space, allowing us to engage with the physical world. Moreover, Jesus's humanity and divinity alter the composition of the body, transforming it from one form to another. Like matter, the body can change from one form to another, such as water turning to vapor and back to liquid. This perspective highlights the dynamic nature of the human body and challenges traditional views that separate the physical and spiritual worlds. By recognizing the interconnectedness of our physical and spiritual selves, we can better understand the depth and breadth of the human experience. The human body is in a constant state of change, with energy conversions occurring continuously based on the body's position and movement. It is not unreasonable to consider the possibility of a conversion of the human body similar to what Jesus underwent, revealing multiple forms of the body in a conceptual space. This perspective challenges traditional views of the human experience and highlights the dynamic nature of the body. By recognizing the interconnectedness of our physical and spiritual selves, we can better understand the potential for growth and transformation within ourselves and our relationship with God.

---

24. "As a human being a person is a whole, not a body without a spirit or a spirit without a body. . . . Thus, the whole unitary person is the object of all God's acts from the bestowal of dominion over the earth to the resurrection of the dead and the end of the world . . . nobody acts with just one part of the self. When somebody thinks, that person actually thinks with the body, and every bodily function is also at the same time a function of the soul and the spirit." A. F. C. Vilmar, quoted in John Kleinig's *Wonderfully Made*, 8.

CONCLUSION

The complexities surrounding Jesus's post-death existence echo themes of guilt, redemption, and controversy depicted in Samuel Coleridge's *Rime of the Ancient Mariner*. Like the mariner burdened by the albatross, Jesus's crucifixion symbolizes sacrifice but can also become a source of scandal and debate, particularly concerning his resurrection.

Various historical texts and philosophical debates challenge the traditional narrative of Jesus's divinity and resurrection, revealing the deep-seated controversies that have persisted over centuries. From the *Toledot Yeshu* to Celsus's assertions, these alternative perspectives reflect efforts to undermine the significance of Jesus's identity and the resurrection event.

However, amidst these debates lies the profound truth of Jesus's resurrection and its transformative power. Through spiritual rebirth, believers are offered the promise of eternal life, transcending the limitations of mortality. Jesus's resurrection serves as a beacon of hope, symbolizing victory over death and offering a path to redemption for humanity.

While questions persist regarding the mysteries of Jesus's birth and resurrection, the Christian understanding emphasizes the unity of divine and human nature in Jesus's personhood. His physical body, transformed yet visible after resurrection, serves as a model for believers' future resurrection and redemption.

In essence, the controversies surrounding Jesus's post-death existence underscore the profound significance of his life, death, and resurrection in shaping religious beliefs.

The exploration of the incarnation of Jesus Christ and the subsequent theological debates about his nature have been pivotal in shaping Christian doctrine. From the early discussions on sinlessness to the councils of Nicaea and Chalcedon, Christians have grappled with understanding how Jesus could be both fully divine and fully human. The Nicene Creed established the essential unity of Christ with the Father, while the Council of Chalcedon affirmed the duality of Christ's nature, remaining perfect in both divinity and humanity.

However, these theological formulations did not occur in isolation. They were influenced by the diverse cultural and philosophical currents of the time, including Greco-Roman, Jewish, and pagan thought. The intersectionality of these influences underscores the complexity of interpreting biblical texts and understanding early Christian beliefs.

Moreover, the examination of Jewish perspectives on the nature of humanity, as well as the comparison with Greek philosophical ideas, provides valuable insights into the broader context of Jesus's teachings. Scholars like Daniel Boyarin and Peter Schäfer have shed light on the fluid boundaries between Judaism and Christianity in the ancient world, highlighting the diversity of beliefs within these traditions.

Furthermore, the concept of intersectionality, as articulated by scholars like Kimberlé Crenshaw, reminds us of the interconnected nature of social categorizations and how they shape religious identities. By considering the multifaceted influences on early Christianity, we can gain a deeper appreciation for the richness and complexity of its theological heritage.

Ultimately, the exploration of the incarnation invites us to delve into profound questions about the nature of humanity and the divine. The virgin conception, as discussed through biblical narratives, rabbinic teachings, and theological interpretations, offers deep-rooted insights into the nature of humanity and the mystery of Christ's incarnation.

The parallels drawn between the virgin births of Jesus and Isaac highlight the theological significance attributed to divine intervention in human birth. Paul's allegorical reading of Sarah's conception of Isaac underscores the symbolic significance of birth through the spirit, contrasting it with birth through the flesh. While modern scholars may not interpret Paul's writings as directly referencing the virgin birth of Jesus, the conceptual framework he presents invites contemplation on the spiritual dimension of human existence.

Moreover, the discussion of body and soul within Jewish and Christian traditions reveals differing perspectives, from a holistic understanding of human existence to dualistic interpretations. The proposal to reconsider the physical embodiment of human beings challenges traditional dualism, emphasizing the inseparability of body and soul and inviting a deeper exploration of the body's role in theological understanding.

Karl Barth's reflection on the mystery of the virgin birth and the empty tomb underscores the limitations of human comprehension in grasping divine truths. His emphasis on the necessity of divine revelation calls for humility and openness in theological inquiry, guided by the work of the Spirit.

Moving forward, there is a call to embrace a holistic understanding of human nature, recognizing the interconnectedness of body and soul. This approach invites further exploration into the mystery of Christ's incarnation and its implications for understanding the whole being of humanity.

In contemplating the spatial dimensions of human existence, from the physical to the spiritual, and the interplay between them, it becomes evident that our understanding of presence extends far beyond mere occupancy of space. Through the lens of various perspectives, from philosophical to theological, we have explored the intricate relationship between body and soul, matter and spirit.

The narrative of Jesus's incarnation, death, and resurrection leads us to take a serious look at the integration of the physical and spiritual realms within human existence. Jesus's transformative journey highlights the potential for the human body to transcend earthly limitations and participate in divine realities.

Moreover, the dynamic nature of the human body, as exemplified by Jesus's own transformation, suggests a continual process of growth and evolution. Just as matter undergoes various forms and energy conversions, so, too, does the human body in its interaction with the spiritual realm.

By embracing this interconnectedness of our physical and spiritual selves, we gain a deeper understanding of the human experience and our relationship with the divine. It invites us to reconsider traditional paradigms and embrace the potential for profound transformation and communion with God.

Ultimately, our journey through space encompasses not only the physical, but also the spiritual dimensions of our being, offering boundless opportunities for exploration, growth, and transcendence.

2

Altering Views of the Body

THE GOSPEL ADDRESSES THE entirety of human existence, encompassing not only the soul but also the body, and not solely the spirit but the complete being. Given the central role of the body in human redemption, resurrection, and the ongoing life of a spiritually renewed individual, it becomes crucial to explore both Jewish and Greek ideologies to enhance our comprehension of Jesus's teachings regarding holistic human nature. The framework of body, soul, and spirit within the early Hellenized Greek church was significantly shaped by philosophers such as Socrates, Plato, and Aristotle. Texts from Plutarch and Philo, referencing Plato's teachings, exhibit contemporaneity with Paul, the Jewish community, and the early Christian community. This suggests a philosophical foundation within Second Temple Judaism and early Christianity. N. T. Wright captures the time surrounding Paul:

> The philosophers were more likely to debate in the marketplace, and that, as well as the synagogue, is where Paul had begun. We hear nothing of the local Jewish reaction; our attention is drawn to the debates with the Epicureans and the Stoics. Here Paul must have been in his element—or rather, one of his elements, since he was obviously at home in the synagogue as well, handling the scriptures with a lifetime's easy fluency. But he was

from Tarsus, one of the main centers of philosophy in the ancient world, and now here he was in Athens, the ultimate homes of learned discourse, the city of Socrates, of Plato, of Aristotle. There was also the "Academy," the ancient school of Plato, which was making a comeback after years of cautious agnosticism.[1]

It can be inferred that Paul was familiar with the philosophical teachings of his non-Jewish contemporaries, particularly those of Plato. In Plato's philosophy, the soul, upon liberation from the body, is prepared for union with its deepest longings: knowledge and wisdom.[2] Guy Stroumsa suggests that early Christian thinkers utilized intellectual tools developed by philosophical schools when engaging with non-Christians, essentially adapting Jewish approaches to the divine into Greek philosophical concepts.[3]

Recognizing the evolving beliefs within Jewish culture that laid the groundwork for the emerging Christian framework, the influence of Greek culture on Christian followers became more evident, especially with the influx of gentile converts influenced by Paul's teachings. Aligning with scholar Daniel Boyarin's perspective, I agree that everyone in the first century, whether accepting Jesus's teachings or not, was inherently connected to Jewish traditions, and the formal emergence of Christianity as a distinct religion occurred later.

A comparative examination of how Jewish and Greek perspectives viewed human existence is essential, given the association of the New Testament gospel with Judaist writers connected to Greek culture. Paul's discussions on Greek philosophy while engaging with Hellenistic Jews highlight parallels between Greek philosophical concepts and teachings found in rabbinic traditions during the early Christian era. The notion of the Hellenization of Christianity is a subset of the broader issue of the impact of Greek language and culture on non-Greek lands after Alexander

---

1. Wright, *Paul: A Biography*, 196–97.
2. Dew and Gould, *Philosophy*, 1.
3. Dew and Gould, *Philosophy*, 47.

the Great's conquests, often referred to as *Hellenism*.[4] The setting for this work is Alexandria, where a Jewish community coexisted with a predominantly gentile population. Despite evident cultural and religious differences, Judaism and Hellenism managed to coexist relatively harmoniously. This resulted in a form of Judaism known as the Judaism of the dispersion, which differed from the Judaism centered around the temple in Jerusalem.[5] However, the Jewish community remained deeply engaged with Scripture until the emergence of the historical and divine figure of Jesus. What's significant is our ability to understand the theology of these communities by examining their interpretation of texts from the Second Temple period through the rabbinical era.

During the Persian and Hellenistic periods, prophecy became literary and continued in a textualized form, and the interpretation of earlier texts became a divinatory act.[6] However, in the face of prophetic decline, Joel prophesied the return of prophecy (Joel 2:28) and proclaimed that Yahweh would again revive prophetic revelations and pour out his Spirit. Later, Peter declares Joel's prophesy to have been fulfilled at Pentecost:

> Peter, standing with the eleven, raised his voice and addressed them, "Men of Judea and all who live in Jerusalem, let this be known to you, and listen to what I say. Indeed, these are not drunk, as you suppose, for it is only nine o'clock in the morning. No, this is what was spoken through the prophet Joel: 'In the last days it will be, God declares, that I will pour out my Spirit upon all flesh, and your sons and your daughters shall prophesy, and your young men shall see visions, and your old men shall dream dreams. Even upon my slaves, both men and women, in those days I will pour out my Spirit; and they shall prophesy.'" (Acts 2:14–18 KJV)

Christians embraced prophetic insights in light of Peter's sermon at Pentecost who interprets the Torah (Ps 16:8–11) to attain a more

---

4. Martens, "Embodiment, Heresy."
5. *OTP* 10.
6. Sharp, *Oxford Handbook of the Prophets*, 15.

THE POWER OF THE RESURRECTED BODY

comprehensive understanding of Jewish perspectives comparing their experiences with that of Christians. Within this Judeo-Christian culture we are led to understand the context of rabbinic Judaism in which lies an oral interpretation of the Torah. As the New Testament was added to the Old Covenant Bible by the church fathers, and formed the basis of their exegesis, so was the Talmud added to the Torah by the rabbis, and formed the special study of later Jewry. The Talmud covers the whole period of the early Christian centuries.[7]

> The origins of rabbinic Judaism are found in the many Judaisms that co-existed during the Second Temple period in the Land of Israel, when biblical and co-biblical texts (Pseudepigrapha, Apocrypha, Dead Sea Scrolls, and others) were edited and interpreted. Classical rabbinic Judaism flourished from the first century CE to the closure of the Babylonian Talmud, c. 600 CE, in Babylonia. Among the different groups of Jews in antiquity, rabbinic Judaism held that at Mount Sinai God revealed the Torah to Moses in two media, the Written and the Oral Torah. The Rabbis claimed they possessed the memorized or Oral Torah.
>
> During the era of Classical Judaism, Rabbis delved into the intricacies of the human body within the Midrash Rabbah, particularly in the book of Genesis.
>
> "The Holy One, blessed be He, said: 'Behold, I will create him from the place of his atonement, and may he endure!'
>
> And He breathed into his nostrils. This teaches that He set him up as a lifeless mass reaching from earth to heaven and then infused a soul into him. (Genesis Rabbah 14:8–9)[8]

In the Hebrew Bible, a distinction is made between spirit and flesh, yet it doesn't align with the kind of dualism seen in Greek

---

7. Mead, *Did Jesus Live 100 B.C.?*, 11.
8. Ulmer, "Brief Introduction," 1.

philosophy, separating the body and soul. Hebrew terms for the soul typically denote an activity or attribute of the body or indicate an entire living being. The holistic being is described as a unified body without its properties being distinct entities. The Hebrew term *nefesh*, commonly translated as "soul," actually means "breath." Meanwhile, *neshamah* occasionally refers specifically to conscious life or intelligence. Additionally, *ruah*, often translated as "spirit," represents powers or actions outside the body and frequently conveys the idea of "wind." By identifying elements that could be easily interpreted as distinct components of the soul—such as breath, spirit, and wind—and applying the same conceptual framework to the body, soul, and spirit, as various parts constituting the entirety of a living being, it becomes reasonable to interpret the text not as suggesting different parts of man's being but rather as describing the components that constitute the entirety of the living being.

Imagine contemplating our existence without the presupposition of being made of separated parts as individuals when considering who we are. We might employ metaphorical terms to comprehend ourselves as living entities, but there would be no division of our essence at life's end. Historically, neither the Hebrews nor Egyptians subscribed to such a notion. The Egyptian Book of the Dead posits that the human soul comprises indivisible components according to various interpretations. While there is no time here to delve into the validity of George James's significant book *Stolen Legacy* (claiming Greek philosophy is borrowed from Egyptian philosophy), James prompts us to compare Egyptian and Greek concepts of body, soul, and spirit.[9] While both Hebrew and Egyptian beliefs encompassed a composite entity comprising a physical and spiritual body, intricately united, Greek philosophy began to separate the components of man's whole being which we will review below. However, Christian theology, believing in life after death, found it natural to adopt Plato's conception of the soul, viewing it as separate from the body. According to Plato, a human

---

9. James, *Stolen Legacy*.

living on earth consists of two parts: soul and body. The soul is the essential part of the human—what makes *me* me.[10]

Against this backdrop, we aim to understand Paul's narratives concerning qualities, forms, and normative representations in which the body presents itself in mixed spaces. The goal is to observe the nature of the body's practices in physical space when the narratives indicate the body is experiencing the material realm, and in spiritual space when the experience is occurring in the Spirit. The mutuality of the body in both spiritual and material realms illustrates the body in its altered forms.

As human beings, individuals are unified entities, encompassing both body and spirit, rather than being merely physical or spiritual entities in isolation. The indivisible person, embodying both aspects, serves as the focal point for all divine actions, highlighting that no action occurs with exclusive consideration of either the body or the spirit alone. This perspective resonates with the views of A. F. C. Vilmar, emphasizing the inseparability of the whole person in God's interactions with humanity.

JESUS'S POSTRESURRECTION APPEARANCE

Ronald J. Sider, in his analysis of St. Paul's conception of the resurrection in I Cor 15:1–19, explores:

> Is interest in the historical factuality of Jesus' alleged resurrection an indication of theological perspicacity or of spiritual unfaithfulness? William R. FARMER has recently argued vehemently that the only kind of evidence for the resurrection the church has ever had-and should have ever desired-is the inner experience of justification by faith alone. To seek any other evidence is to believe in a God of Magic, who is some "celestial sleight-of-hand artist" rather than the true God. BARTH and BULTMANN, too, are typical of many who, albeit in somewhat different ways, reject any citation of historical evidence to support the church's belief in Jesus' resurrection. The

---

10. Swinburne, "Soul, Nature."

writings of people like Richard R. NIEBUHR and Wolfhart PANNENBERG, however, demonstrate that no consensus exists apropos the advisability of concern about the historicity of Jesus' resurrection.[11]

Contrary to the scholars suggesting that Paul, unlike the Gospels, posited Jesus's resurrected body as purely spiritual, I argue otherwise. First, to accept that Jesus's resurrected body was spiritual necessitates belief in his postresurrection appearances being nonphysical—an assertion contradicted by Paul in I Cor 15. Second, the idea that Paul considered Jesus's resurrected body merely a future template for all resurrected bodies, thus rendering it spiritual, lacks factual basis. While the resurrected body may serve as a model, Paul implies in 2 Cor 12:1–4 that the human body can transcend temporal boundaries, suggesting it cannot be confined to a purely spiritual realm. Therefore, dismissing the physical body as purely spiritual necessitates considering it an interpolation at minimum. Further arguments against Paul's acceptance of a physical resurrected body hinge on contextual considerations—whether Paul was addressing Hellenist Jews, gnostics, or ancient Jewish believers. While this may shed light on why Paul frames his argument as he does, closer scrutiny should be directed not only to the beginning but also to the conclusion of Paul's discourse, where his position becomes clearer.

The significance of Jesus's body lies in its revelation of the profound mystery surrounding our personal identity. This revelation is crucial because it unveils that the body transcends being merely a physical entity confined to the dimensions of time and space. Instead, it emphasizes the transformative nature of Jesus's body, seamlessly transitioning between divine and human forms from birth to resurrection.

In previous books and articles, I characterized the human body as a representational phenomenon, emphasizing interconnected components that collectively form a unified entity. The entirety of the body, shaped by Jesus, is posited to exist on both spiritual and material planes, suggesting an inherent design to

---

11. Sider, "St. Paul's Understanding," 124.

bridge the gap between the invisible, eternal realm of God, and the visible, temporal realm of his creation. This perspective implies that human bodies transcend limitations solely within this world, also belonging to the eternal realm of God. The significance of this concept is notably underscored in discussions about the resurrected body.

In Christianity, the resurrected body is often associated with the transformative nature of life after death, drawing from the resurrection of Jesus Christ. Theological discourse explores aspects like incorruptibility, imperishability, and spiritualization of the body. As we have shown above, comparisons and contrasts with other religious views on the afterlife and resurrected bodies also contribute to a comprehensive understanding of this concept. This belief is rooted in biblical passages, such as 1 Cor 15, where the apostle Paul discusses the nature of the resurrected body:

> For I handed on to you as of first importance what I in turn had received: that Christ died for our sins in accordance with the scriptures, and that he was buried, and that he was raised on the third day in accordance with the scriptures, and that he appeared to Cephas, then to the twelve. Then he appeared to more than five hundred brothers and sisters at one time, most of whom are still alive, though some have died. Then he appeared to James, then to all the apostles. (1 Cor 15:3–7)

Paul endeavors to establish the tangible reality of Jesus's postresurrection presence by emphasizing that he was seen, touched, held, and embraced by many. In contemplating Jesus's appearance following his death, believers catch a glimpse of the future body awaiting all who accept him as their savior. The resurrection transformation is immediate and precedes the ultimate transformation of the world. Bodily transformation aligns with an eschatology that focuses on rebirth and the migration of new believers toward the culmination of time. In his resurrected body, Jesus is both human and divine, two natures being present at the same time. The new body of Jesus raised by the Spirit completes the resurrection of humans, not at the culmination of time (eschatology), but here on earth. Like both Hebrew and Egyptian beliefs, humans are comprised of a physical and spiritual body, intricately united.

In Christianity, an eschatological perspective traditionally envisions an afterlife in the new heaven and earth, with a primary emphasis on apocalyptic judgment. However, Paul, in 1 Cor 15, advocates for a nuanced eschatology that envisions the body transcending beyond the constraints of time, space, and matter, before the culmination of time. This perspective invites believers to consider a realm beyond the earthly, aligning with the transformative nature of resurrection.

> But someone will ask, "How are the dead raised? With what kind of body do they come?" Fool! What you sow does not come to life unless it dies. And as for what you sow, you do not sow the body that is to be, but a bare seed, perhaps of wheat or of some other grain. But God gives it a body as he has chosen, and to each kind of seed its own body. Not all flesh is alike, but there is one flesh for human beings, another for animals, another for birds, and another for fish. There are both heavenly bodies and earthly bodies, but the glory of the heavenly is one thing, and that of the earthly is another. (1 Cor 15:35–41)

Herein lies the analogy: the earthly body serves as the bare seed of the immortal body. To truly grasp the depth of Paul's discourse on the body, we must avoid imposing our contemporary perspectives onto the text. It is tempting, given our modern context, to dissect the physical body from the entirety of the human being, leading to the misconception that a part of the individual has perished. However, what Paul says in the preceding verses he underscores in 2 Cor 5:17, "Therefore, if anyone is in Christ, he is a new creation: old things are passed away; behold, all things are become new" (KJV). This encapsulates the essence of Paul's teaching on the transformative nature of being united with Christ, wherein believers undergo a profound metamorphosis in their new life without shedding the identity and existence of their natural being.

Considering this truth, it becomes evident why we affirm Christ's resurrection on earth, as witnessed by the apostles and numerous others. Christ possesses a recognizable yet transformed body, no longer constrained by physical limitations, spatial boundaries, or temporal constraints.

Referring back to Paul's polemical questions, "How are the dead raised? With what kind of body do they come?" we see an emphasis on the transformation of the material body, signaling its readiness for existence in the new world at the resurrection. During early Christianity, Jewish beliefs about resurrection aligned closely with Paul's viewpoint, whereas the Greeks found the concept unimaginable. Despite potential objections to the idea of the natural body retaining its characteristics, Paul provides reassurance that the present body will undergo resurrection as a transformed one.

The New Testament is rich with scriptural references to the resurrection, and in Rom 8, Paul employs a combination of apocalyptic eschatology language and a realized eschatology emphasizing new life in the present. He asserts that the indwelling of Christ within individuals brings life to mortal bodies through the Spirit. This dual perspective underscores Paul's eschatological teaching, which involves the resurrection of the body to a mediated place beyond the constraints of time, space, and matter.

In the Pauline letters, a consistent theme emerges, highlighting a profound transformation from darkness to light within the human experience on earth. This transformation involves the cessation of the old self (pre-union with Christ) and the resurrection of a new self (post-union with Christ). The notion of a perishing individual is apparent. If the spiritual body undergoes a transformative experience leading to the cessation of the old spiritual man, we should not attribute a lesser standard to the physical body. As the identity and existence of the former spiritual body conclude, it surprisingly continues to flourish on earth. Consequently, the physical body must also reach its end and endure in thriving during the afterlife. Subsequently, he clarifies that mortality will transition into immortality, as the perishable embraces the imperishable. Once again, Paul introduces the concept of transformation, always enveloped in mystery.

Paul asserts that a transformative process must precede the perishable taking on the imperishable and the mortal attaining immortality. Followers of his teachings are promised "new bodies" that can exist simultaneously in both the spiritual and physical realms. The spiritual body is presented as a conceptual counterpart to the earthly body, creating a dual illusion where the spiritual body is concealed beneath the earthly one.[12] In these verses, Paul implies the dual nature of humanity before and after resurrection.

Before delving deeper into the resurrection and the perspective on the body in the afterlife, it is crucial to acknowledge that Paul does not delay in suggesting that the present body closely resembles the resurrected one and is not confined by spatial boundaries. This insight is coupled with his accounts of encounters with otherworldly companions.

In 2 Cor 12:2-7, Paul shares an experience of encountering a man during a journey to the third heaven. The ambiguity of whether he was "in" or "out" of the body implies a possible separation of the soul from the body. Because Paul's ministry was to Hellenists, his teachings on the resurrection and immortality were somehow intertwined with Hellenistic philosophy and the continued development of a Jewish eschatological belief. Herein there is a similarity between these passages in Paul and Plato's stories about a person raptured away to paradise who sees incredible visions and hears mystical messages.[13] Plato shares the story of Er in the book *Republic*:

> The philosopher uses the story to illustrate the lasting importance for people to live right and practice justice (Plato, *Resp.* 10.614d-619b). Plato seeks to demonstrate that despite how great the prizes, gifts, and rewards a righteous person might receive here on earth, they fail to compare—in both number and magnitude—with what awaits them after death (Plato, *Resp.* 10.614a). As the story goes, Er is a valiant warrior who dies in battle. After he is slain, it takes his friends twelve days to find

---

12. Evans, *Holy Spirit as Space*, 19.
13. Briones and Dodson, *Paul and the Giants*, 135.

his body, deliver it home, and prepare for the funeral. On that last day, his loved ones place Er's corpse on a pyre to incinerate it. And yet, as they are getting ready to light it on fire, Er sits up. He shocks the crowd by coming back to life. Er actually details what he saw "in the world beyond." According to Er, at the beginning of his twelve-day journey in the afterlife, the judges gathered him together with the other departed souls around the judgment seat. But over against the rest, Er gets a pass. Rather than remaining with the dead, the judges appoint him to take a look around and take notes so that he can go back and give a report to humanity regarding the destiny of the dead.[14]

Drawing a comparison to Plato's tale of Er in the *Republic*, Paul returns to earth after a celestial encounter, urging believers onward. This crucial concept underscores the notion that, rather than conforming to the prevalent belief of eradicating human mortality, Paul advocates for the transformation of the mortal into the immortal. The mortal body evolves as a seed for the immortal body, mirroring the way the former spiritual body served as a seed for the emerging spiritual form.

THE NATURE OF THE RESURRECTED BODY

The Jewish apocalypses delve into the temporal transcendence, contemplating the fate of the deceased, whether it entails the punishment of the wicked or the vindication of the righteous. They seek to answer the question, What happens to the wicked and the righteous when they die? (cf. 1 En. 22:1–14; 94:6–104:8[38]).[15]

In 2 Cor 12:1–9, Paul makes reference to multiple heavens, suggesting either the immortality of the soul or a recognized separation of body and soul. This stands in contrast to the notion proposed by some scholars that Paul solely anticipated the return of Christ, believing in an afterlife confined to earth.

---

14. Briones and Dodson, *Paul and the Giants*, 136–37.
15. Reynolds, *Jewish Apocalyptic Tradition*, 6.

N. T. Wright reflects on his early studies, noting that the concept of souls departing to heaven was more aligned with Platonist ideals like those of Plutarch rather than Christian beliefs of Paul's time. He suggests that the framework of *heaven and hell* taken for granted today emerged much later, particularly in the High Middle Ages, with later reformers adding their own interpretations, which differed significantly from the perspectives of the first century.[16]

Across various apocalyptic texts such as Ezra, Daniel, and 1 Enoch, Jesus's words in the Gospels, and in the writings of Paul and Peter, there are descriptions of otherworldly experiences suggesting a connection between the human spirit (or soul) and a realm beyond time, space, and matter. However, within the rabbinic tradition there was a different emphasis, with no pressing need to define the nature of the resurrection body due to the expectation of earthly continuation upon the arrival of the messiah, unlike in Christianity where the concept of the immortality of the soul was significant.

Before his conversion to Christianity, the apostle Paul, once a devout Pharisee from Tarsus, was immersed in the cultural, philosophical, and religious milieu of ancient Greece and Rome. His writings offer glimpses into an eschatological Christian view where humans transition to a new heaven and earth. While some scholars interpret Paul's letters as advocating for a renewal theology, others align his teachings with a belief in the restoration of heaven and earth as the final dwelling place for humanity, a view paralleled in John's Revelation.

Despite limited research on the intermediate state of the soul after death concerning Paul's eschatology, there is sufficient evidence within his New Testament letters to construct an eschatological perspective influenced by Judean teachings and resonating with some principles of Plato's philosophy. Paul's understanding of the resurrection prior to his conversion would have been shaped by Pharisaic beliefs within the Greco-Roman context of the first century.

---

16. Wright, *Paul: A Biography*, 8.

Paul's apocalyptic ideas about the spirit world were rooted in Old Testament Judaism, Hellenistic thought, and his own mystical experiences. It is evident that Paul's theological beliefs and evolving eschatology, including his understanding of the afterlife, were partly molded by the cultural setting of his time.

In contrast, the Hebrew Bible describes the soul of the deceased person entering Sheol upon death, which is often interpreted as the grave. In this conception, both body and soul enter Hades, echoing themes found in Greek literature such as the *Odyssey*, ancient Greek epic poems attributed to Homer. The Underworld, or simply *Hades*, is portrayed as the domain ruled by the god of the dead.

Regarding the body, it does not lie in the tomb lacking the ability or strength to move, for through prayers and rituals during burial, it is imbued with the ability to transform into a *sāu*, or spiritual body. Phrases like "I germinate like the plants" and "My flesh germinateth" signify this transformation, suggesting a body endowed with knowledge, power, and incorruptibility. This transformed body has the capacity to commune with the soul, ascend to heaven, and dwell with the divine and the righteous souls.[17]

Prior to the book of Isaiah, there is no account of an afterlife. In Third Isaiah (Isa 56–66), there emerges talk of a transformed heaven and earth. Given that both the body and the soul enter Sheol, the subsequent doctrine of resurrection, as articulated in passages like Isa 24–27 and Dan 12, suggests a return to life in both aspects. This underscores the significance of our study above, which delineates the components comprising the entirety of the living being. Both the mortal body and the spiritual component thereof play integral roles in the transition of the living being from temporal to eternal existence.

The first definite appearance in Jewish thought of a doctrine of personal survival of death in a general resurrection of the dead comes in the literature associated with the Hasmonean

---

17. Budge, *Egyptian Book of the Dead*, 66.

Revolt (166–64 BCE), from which time it increases in importance to become a central dogma, later a part of the basic doctrine of Christianity.[18]

Traditionally, ancient Israel did not have a hope of eternal life beyond their present existence. In Judaism, everyone, irrespective of behavior or social status, descended to Sheol, the dark underworld where one was cut off from God's presence, and lived a quasi-life there.[19] But the idea of individual resurrection, which occurs in the Hebrew Bible for the first time in Daniel, introduced a kind of hope for the future that was radically new in the context of Jewish tradition.[20]

The Jewish tradition offers instances where individuals close to God or serving him were taken up to heaven by God, even before the concepts of bodily resurrection or spiritual immortality were articulated. For instance, Enoch's story illustrates this: "Enoch walked with God; then he was no more, because God took him" (Gen 5:24). Hebrews 11:5 further confirms Enoch's exceptional fate, stating that "By faith Enoch was taken so that he did not experience death." Likewise, Elijah's departure is described in 2 Kgs 2:11, where "a chariot of fire and horses of fire separated the two of them, and Elijah ascended in a whirlwind into heaven."

These accounts suggest that bodily ascension into heaven was a reality in the Jewish tradition, similar to the concept of bodily resurrection that emerged during the Second Temple period and evolved within Christianity.

The Christian motif of an eternal life theology seems to have started with a Jewish belief in apocalyptic writings. Still, some Jewish sects like the Sadducees did not accept the motif of resurrection, and those who did believe in resurrection did not give up their beliefs about fulfillment on earth. Eventually, following Christ's death, Christians looked for the parousia.

During the Hellenistic and early Roman periods, new ideas about the afterlife begin to develop within Judaism and

18. Bemporad, "Soul: Jewish Concept."
19. Collins, *Short Introduction*, 84.
20. Collins, *Short Introduction*, 518.

Christianity, for a number of reasons. In particular, Hellenism allowed for greater exposure to ideas from other cultures.[21] Christianity came to terms with the continued existence of the world, and it incorporated two conceptions that were quite foreign to its original formulation—the immortality of the soul and an interim state in which the soul exists until the Savior arrives to judge the world.[22] Alan Segal suggests that the Hellenistic environment contributed to the Hebrews' development of the resurrection and immortality of the soul.

What is to be considered is that there is an implicit ambiguity in the word *soul*. Though the soul terminology may suggest to us the Greek notion of immortal souls, it is more likely that the Hebrew word *nefesh* alone is understood here as the principle of identity for the martyrs in the intermediary state between their deaths and their resurrection. It is however important that the soul language was developed to help serve the purpose of justifying the martyrs, explaining where they reside until the consummation.[23] Even at that, we must consider Moses and Elijah who appear to Jesus as if they were occupying an intermediate state.

However, the lack of eschatological doctrine was a weakness of Christianity. In contrast, Judaism drew strength from its anticipation of a future kingdom, as evidenced in the Old Testament literature. The emergence of a parousia doctrine during the medieval age contributed to the contemporary appreciation of early Christianity's eschatology. Early church fathers interpreted Jesus's reference to paradise (*paradeisos*) (Luke 23:43) as a realm that predated the fall and now transcends the present world. Embracing the belief in a future existence in such a place bolsters the faith of Christians and encourages them to relinquish earthly desires that hinder their relationship with God or one day inhabiting heaven.

However, if the argument presented throughout this study holds true, the foundation of a future eschatology hinges on a present eschatological event in Christ, necessitating transformation in

---

21. Henning, "Hell."
22. Segal, *Life After Death*, 486.
23. Segal, *Life After Death*, 485.

the present moment. Scholars have long contemplated the concept of the eschatological event occurring in the *now* and *not yet*, where heaven and earth converge in the present, while the ultimate resurrection of the Christ event awaits his return in the future. This pivotal "Christ event" occurs when the living Christ is unveiled to humanity through what is termed as special revelation. The Holy Spirit serves as the mediator between two realms, bridging the temporal and eternal dimensions, and operating within both the divine and natural realms to actualize this profound transformation of the whole being.

In summary, when discussing the human being, we are considering the entirety of the individual. However, when examining specific aspects or parts of this whole, it is not to imply that these parts can function independently or exist separately from the cohesive functioning of all elements both before and after any resurrection. This perspective underscores that the natural and spiritual aspects of the human body—distinctly referenced here for clarity—operate in tandem; they are not capable of operating autonomously from each other. Thus, when discussing the body as a dual entity, it is because both its natural and spiritual dimensions are intricately interwoven, forming an inseparable unity.

MULTIPLE ELEMENTS OF THE RESURRECTED BODY

The ideas concerning the resurrected body in rabbinic Judaism and ancient Egyptian beliefs bear resemblances to early Christian thought influenced by Hellenistic concepts. Paul emerges as a significant figure in shaping the New Testament's outlook on the body, presenting a compelling interpretation of the transformed being, which I suggest manifests as a spatial entity. Whereas the physical body maintains a close relationship with the natural world, the spiritual body, linked with the soul, has connections to the realm of the Spirit. This perspective enables us to view the body as a dual phenomenon, comprising both spiritual and physical dimensions. Each aspect evolves simultaneously, yet remains hidden from the other within their respective environments.[24] The spatial aspect of the body fits into elements used in Jewish, Egyptian, and Greek literature. Herein life is characterized by the fact that the living entity differentiates itself from the world in which it exists while remaining interconnected, preserving its own identity through this differentiation. The essence of being alive lies in the assimilation of the external. Differentiation, therefore, simultaneously entails a sense of nondifferentiation, as the foreign is internalized and appropriated.[25]

Herein the unified existence of an individual has many parts. This unified being reflects the holistic nature of the embodied Hebrew individual, encompassing elements such as *nephesh, neshamah,* and *ruah*. Similarly, the Egyptian understanding of the body includes components like *ka, khat, ba, kaibit, khu, sekhem, sahu,* and *ren*.

To fully comprehend the conceptual framework of the body, it is essential to juxtapose Hebrew and Egyptian perspectives with New Testament theology. Terms often considered metaphorical should be interpreted more literally, with slight adjustments. For instance, when Paul refers to believers as "the temple of the Holy Spirit," it is plausible to suggest that he is drawing a parallel between the Holy Spirit and the Hebrew concept of *ruah*, akin to the wind, as well as likening the body to a house.

In the Gospels, the portrayal of the body as a shelter for elements of the soul appears to extend beyond mere metaphor. For instance, in Matt 12:29, the analogy of the body as a house for the human being is presented: "Or how can one enter a strong man's house and plunder his property, without first tying up the strong man? Then indeed the house can be plundered." Similarly, Matt 12:43 suggests that the body hosts occupants beyond just the human soul: "When the unclean spirit has gone out of a person, it wanders through waterless regions looking for a resting place, but it finds none. Then it says, 'I will return to my house from which I came.' When it comes, it finds it empty, swept, and put in order.

24. Evans, *Holy Spirit as Space*, 128.
25. Evans, *Holy Spirit as Space*, 127.

Then it goes and brings along seven other spirits more evil than itself, and they enter and live there; and the last state of that person is worse than the first."

The idea of multiple entities coexisting within a single human being is grounded in the understanding of humans as spatial beings. This notion is in harmony with the belief that the Father and Son can establish a connection with individuals from within their own beings, as described in John 14:23: "Jesus answered him, 'Those who love me will keep my word, and my Father will love them, and we will come to them and make our home with them.'"

Considering the body as a boundary that accommodates living entities, much like a residence fostering a cohesive community, implies that different facets of human makeup can be seen as a shared dwelling. This perspective resonates with the analogy of temples, echoing Paul's portrayal in I Cor 6:19–20: "Or do you not know that your body is a temple of the Holy Spirit within you, which you have from God, and that you are not your own? For you were bought with a price; therefore glorify God in your body." Does this Scripture not imply a literal interpretation, aligning with Jesus's words, "Destroy this temple, and in three days I will raise it up"? The Jews then remarked, "'This temple has been under construction for forty-six years, and will you raise it up in three days?' But he was referring to the temple of his body" (John 2:19–21). As spatial beings, we inhabit multiple spaces simultaneously. Could it be that all believers collectively inhabit Jesus's body? Do they not all partake in the communion between the Father and the Son within their dwelling? Or is it not the Holy Spirit that unites all believers within the Lord's temple?

Now, let us delve into an exploration of the components of man's complete being before delving into the entities that inhabit it. Expanding further on this analogy, the Egyptian concept of *ka*, characterized by an abstract personality with autonomous existence, possesses the ability to traverse locations freely, opting to either separate from or merge with the body as desired. Belief in such capabilities finds resonance in the narratives of Jesus's exorcisms of demons in the Gospels, where spirits take residence in the body, can be expelled, yet persist in returning if no other entity takes up residence.

Ultimately, the distinction between the Egyptian *ka* and Hellenistic thought lies in the *ka's* role as an integral element of the whole being, whereas Hellenistic philosophy tends to separate the soul from the body after death. However, scholar George James, in *Stolen Legacy*, identifies this belief not with the Egyptian *ka*, which is inseparable from its whole being, but rather with Aristotle's explication of the soul. As James observes, says Mary Lefkowitz, Aristotle wrote a treatise *On the Soul*; the Egyptians believed in the immortality of the soul. But there the similarity ends. James admits that there is no close resemblance, because Aristotle's theory is only a "very small portion" of the Egyptian "philosophy" of the soul, as described in the Egyptian Book of the Dead.[26] Below is a concept of the soul in relation to the Egyptian belief.

> The Ka, an abstract personality with autonomous existence, can freely traverse locations, choosing to separate from or unite with the body at will. The soul has nine parts, whose unity is so complete, that even the Ren, i.e., the name, is an essential attribute, since without it, it cannot exist. The Khat represents the mortal and susceptible-to-decay physical body. The Ba, akin to the heart, embodies the essential life force in a person and can alter its form as desired. The Kaibit is the shadow of an individual, connected with the Ba (heart and soul), and, like the Ka, possesses independence, capable of movement. The Khu signifies the immortal spirit in man. The Sekhem stands for the power or form of man as a formidable force. The Sahu is a body that has attained a level of knowledge, power, and glory, transforming into an incorruptible state. The Ren symbolizes man as a celestial being.[27]

All these were, however, bound together inseparably, and the welfare of any single one of them concerned the welfare of all. For the well being of the spiritual parts it was necessary to preserve from

---

26. Lefkowitz, "Myth of a 'Stolen Legacy,'" 104.
27. James, *Stolen Legacy*, 103–4.

decay the natural body; and certain passages in the pyramid texts seem to show that a belief in the resurrection of the natural body existed in the earliest dynasties.[28] This reflection coincides with the Hebrew belief that the whole person descends to Hades (the grave).

There is, however, no doubt that from first to last the Egyptians firmly believed that besides the soul there was some other element of the man that would rise again. The preservation of the corruptible body, too, was in some way connected with the life in the world to come, and its preservation was necessary to ensure eternal life.[29] Still, Egyptian belief in the corruptible body being resurrected from the dead is absent. This too might explain why Aristotle focused on the soul's passage to the afterlife.

Nevertheless, George James contends that specific facets of the Aristotelian understanding of the soul function autonomously from the body. This notion resonates with the philosophical perspectives of Plato and, consequently, aligns with Paul's discourse on the soul.

However, Paul does not argue for the separation of the soul from the body. Instead, he contextualizes his teachings within the framework of Hellenistic thought, drawing from philosophical discourse, while also reintroducing Jewish teachings concerning the unity of the whole being. In doing so, he presents a critique of Plato's philosophy, which accentuated the pursuit of knowledge and wisdom as a means to ready the soul for its ultimate union with the eternal and transcendent realm of forms.[30]

Before experiencing transformation in Jesus and the renewal of the Holy Spirit, Paul refers to various elements of the body as members of the body in Romans:

> For we know that the law is spiritual; but I am of the flesh, sold into slavery under sin. I do not understand my own actions. For I do not do what I want, but I do the very thing I hate. Now if I do what I do not want, I agree that the law is good. But in fact, it is no longer I

28. Budge, *Egyptian Book of the Dead*, 59.
29. Budge, *Egyptian Book of the Dead*, 65.
30. Evans, *Holy Spirit as Space*, 88.

> that do it, but sin that dwells within me. For I know that nothing good dwells within me, that is, in my flesh. I can will what is right, but I cannot do it. For I do not do the good I want, but the evil I do not want is what I do. Now if I do what I do not want, it is no longer I that do it, but sin that dwells within me.
>
> So I find it to be a law that when I want to do what is good, evil lies close at hand. For I delight in the law of God in my inmost self, but I see in my members another law at war with the law of my mind, making me captive to the law of sin that dwells in my members. Wretched man that I am! Who will rescue me from this body of death? Thanks be to God through Jesus Christ our Lord! (Rom 7:14–25)

Here, we observe different parts of our being functioning independently but impacting the whole body. The conflicting actions between his heart (innermost self) where he has hidden the word of God (law) and an existential part of his being (law of sin) also housed in the body. Sin proves too powerful and defeats his intention. Because of his lack of power, Paul confesses that he resides in a body of death. It is not until the subsequent chapter that Paul introduces complete deliverance from the dead body to which he has been captive.

Paul's understanding suggests that the resurrected body maintains its fundamental characteristics while undergoing transformation through the influence of the Spirit. Examining the different ways in which the resurrected body undergoes change helps us better grasp the nature of its transformation.

Revisiting the notion of the soul in the context of Paul's defense influenced by Plato, we further explore the parallels between Hebrew and Greek perspectives on the constituents of the complete being. In Egyptian beliefs, the *ba* intertwines with the *kaibit*, the heart, and the soul, aligning with what Christians identify as the inner self. In Eph 3:16, Paul prays for strength in the inner man, which represents the heart of the human being and is also perceived as the spiritual aspect of humans, contrasting with the outward man, or body. Similarly, the Hebrew term *nefesh*, often translated as "soul," actually signifies breath, aligning with the concepts mentioned above. Moreover, *neshamah* occasionally denotes conscious life or intelligence, further alluding to the soul. The *khu*, representing the immortal spirit, corresponds to Paul's references to the spiritual man. In 2 Cor 5:17, Paul declares, "So if anyone is in Christ, there is a new creation: everything old has passed away; see, everything has become new!" *Sekhem* denotes the power or force inherent in humans, differing from *ruah* in that its influence extends outward, akin to the force of the wind. The Egyptians elucidated this concept further through the term *sahu*, which signifies maturity and attainment of knowledge, power, and glory, leading to a state of incorruptibility. Last, the *ren* symbolizes humans as celestial beings.

Clearly, the Egyptian concept of these elements of the body are not confined to the same spatial dimensions but possess the ability to operate independently while maintaining their cohesion within the whole. But of importance is that simultaneously they illustrate the body's capacity to undergo transformation across various spaces, whether temporal or eternal, reflecting contrasting perspectives of the natural world versus heavenly realms.

The heart is the inner part of man and David, in Ps 64:6, suggests that the heart is deep. Remember, in Hebrew thought the heart designates the most inward part of a person, the center of one's will and thoughts. In a poetic fashion, when David speaks of the heart and soul in the same verses of Psalms, he is only referring to himself as a whole. Therefore, the heart is not the center mass for the body, but a phenomena composed of the emotions, thoughts, and acts of a person. The phenomena of thoughts and feelings and actions that have been filtered through experience becomes a part of the heart of man's being at the center.

In the work *A Handbook on the Gospel of Mark* by Robert G. Bratcher and Eugene A. Nida, the passage Mark 12:30, "And you shall love the Lord your God with all your heart and with all your soul and with all your mind and with all your strength," demonstrates variations in perceived text:

> In many languages one cannot "love with the heart." For example, in Kabba-Laka one must love with the liver; in Conob the equivalent expression is "abdomen"; in the Marshallese one can love with the throat. The heart is thus translated by a number of other terms which represent the emotional center or focus of the personality.
>
> *Soul* is generally translated in two ways: (1) by means of words which identify that part of the personality which lives on after death, often called the "shadow" or "the counterpart" and (2) by means of terms for "life," "insides," or "person." In this context the latter meaning is involved, e.g. "love the Lord your God with all your heart and with all your life" (Kiyaka). In Navajo the living soul is "that which stands inside of one."
>
> *Mind* may be translatable in some languages only as "thoughts," since the mind as separate from thoughts is not recognized.[31]

Indeed, Christians have embraced an integrated dualism, but is it what impedes us from exploring deeper into the composite nature of humanity, extending beyond the conventional notions of body and soul? This limited interpretation often disregards the insights offered by the apocalyptic writings of the Hebrew Bible and the potential influences from the Hellenistic culture of the first century, as alluded to in Paul's Platonic themes.

The multifaceted aspects of the body, seen as a unified entity, are not always clearly distinguished. There exists a subtle disparity between Jewish literature and New Testament letters, compounded by reluctance in interpreting the latter in light of the former's apocalyptic writings. Apocalyptic texts imply the body's occupancy in both physical and spiritual realms. In Jewish belief, the deceased persist in their entirety, including their bodies, within Sheol (the grave). Despite Christianity introducing the concept of an afterlife in heaven, the understanding of humanity's bodily existence beyond death remains somewhat ambiguous.

Nonetheless, evolving perspectives on the body, particularly in comparison to Jesus's resurrected body on earth, can reinforce

---

31. Bratcher and Nida, *Handbook on the Gospel of Mark*, 383.

the belief in the resurrection of the entire being, akin to that of Jesus'. Reflecting on Jesus's resurrection, a comprehensive analysis of apocalyptic writings in both the Old and New Testaments presents further avenues for understanding life beyond death as an integrated whole, including the body.

CONCLUSION

From the Judaic roots intertwining with Greek philosophy to the evolving perspectives within early Christianity, our comprehension of the holistic nature of humanity deepens.

The journey through history reveals a dynamic dialogue between different cultural and philosophical frameworks, each contributing to our understanding of the human condition. From Paul's engagement with Greek philosophy to the synthesis of Jewish and Hellenistic thought in early Christian communities, we witness the ongoing evolution of theological discourse.

Central to this exploration is the recognition of the human body as more than just a physical vessel, but as an integral aspect of our spiritual and existential reality. Whether through Jewish midrashic interpretations or Platonic dualism, diverse perspectives converge to affirm the interconnectedness of body, soul, and spirit.

Furthermore, the fluidity of the human experience across physical and spiritual realms underscores the unity of the individual as a composite entity. As we navigate through mixed spaces, we embody the fullness of our being, engaging with both the material and the divine.

Ultimately, our understanding of the body transcends mere physicality, encompassing the spiritual dimensions of our existence. Through this holistic lens, we come to appreciate the profound depth and complexity of the human body, a vessel through which we encounter the divine and participate in the unfolding narrative of creation.

While scholars may debate the significance of seeking historical evidence versus relying solely on inner experience for belief in the resurrection, the richness of Paul's teachings in 1 Cor 15 invites us to delve deeper.

Contrary to some interpretations, Paul's writings suggest a profound affirmation of the physicality of Jesus's resurrected body, emphasizing its tangible reality through eyewitness accounts and encounters. This understanding not only underscores the authenticity of Jesus's resurrection but also holds profound implications for our understanding of personal identity and the nature of existence.

Paul's teachings point to a transformative process wherein the mortal body is transformed into an immortal one, bridging the gap between the earthly and the divine. This transformative journey, depicted as a transition from darkness to light, entails a profound metamorphosis that extends beyond mere physicality to encompass the entirety of one's being.

Moreover, Paul's encounters with otherworldly realms, reminiscent of Platonic narratives, further emphasize the continuity and transformation of the human experience beyond the confines of earthly existence. Through these encounters, Paul elucidates the interconnectedness of the spiritual and the physical, highlighting the transcendent nature of the resurrected body.

Paul's teachings on the resurrection challenge us to reconsider our conceptions of the body, mortality, and immortality. They invite us to embrace a nuanced understanding of eschatology that envisions a future where the limitations of time, space, and matter are transcended, and the fullness of our existence is realized in union with Christ. In embracing this transformative vision, we are called to participate in the ongoing renewal of creation, anticipating the culmination of all things in the new heaven and earth.

The exploration of the nature of the resurrected body traverses a complex tapestry of theological, philosophical, and cultural threads. From ancient Jewish apocalyptic writings to early Christian interpretations, from Hellenistic influences to rabbinic traditions, the discourse surrounding the afterlife and the resurrection body is rich and varied.

Key figures like the apostle Paul offer insights into the evolving eschatological perspectives of their time, drawing from diverse sources to articulate their understanding of the transition from earthly existence to eternal life. Concepts such as the immortality of the soul, bodily resurrection, and the interim state between death and judgment emerge against the backdrop of cultural exchange and theological reflection.

Throughout history, different religious traditions have grappled with the fundamental question of what happens to the human being after death. From the ancient Hebrew belief in Sheol to the Christian hope in a resurrected body, from the Greek concept of an immortal soul to the Jewish expectation of a future kingdom, diverse perspectives converge and diverge, each contributing to the mosaic of human understanding.

Yet, amidst this diversity, a common thread emerges—the interconnectedness of the natural and spiritual dimensions of the human body. Whether described as a transformed body capable of communion with the divine or as a spiritual entity transcending earthly constraints, the resurrected body is depicted as integral to the continuity of personal identity and the fulfillment of eschatological hope.

The exploration of the nature of the resurrected body invites us to ponder the mystery of human existence and the profound implications of faith for our understanding of life, death, and eternity. It challenges us to embrace the tension between the present reality and the future promise, between the earthly and the heavenly, as we journey toward the fulfillment of God's ultimate purpose for creation.

Our exploration challenges conventional interpretations. From rabbinic Judaism to ancient Egyptian beliefs, and from Hellenistic influences to early Christian thought, we've encountered a diverse array of perspectives.

Central to our discussion is the notion of the body as a dual phenomenon, comprising both spiritual and physical dimensions. This understanding allows us to appreciate the interconnectedness of different aspects of human existence, from the *nephesh*, *neshamah,* and *ruah* in Hebrew thought to the *ka, khat, ba,* and other components in Egyptian beliefs.

Paul's contributions to New Testament theology offer a compelling interpretation of the transformed being, emphasizing the continuity and transformation of the body through the influence of the Spirit. His writings challenge us to reconsider traditional dichotomies and embrace a more integrated understanding of human nature.

Examining biblical passages alongside philosophical discourse and apocalyptic writings sheds light on the complex nature of the human being and its destiny beyond death. While interpretations may vary, the overarching theme of unity and transformation persists, urging us to delve deeper into the mysteries of existence.

3

Resurrecting the Body

IF WE ENTERTAIN THE notion that the body merely functions as a vessel for the human embryo, it implies that humanity dwells within a dystopian society orchestrated by a divine authority, under perpetual surveillance and plagued by the fear of a cataclysmic end. This concept bears striking resemblance to the premise of the *Matrix*, a simulated reality wherein humans are tethered to a world controlled by machines, their experiences predetermined, rendering choice illusory, with answers preordained.

In the *Matrix* trilogy, the protagonist Neo's corporeal form isn't his actual flesh-and-blood body but rather a digital construct known as a "residual self-image," shaped by his mind. The demise of their Matrix avatars spells the demise of their physical bodies and vice versa. But Neo, as the chosen one, encounters death and rebirth within the Matrix, burdened with the task of liberating others from its societal confines and cultural indoctrination. For those who break free to the real world, depicted in the narrative, gain the ability to shape their destinies, seek truth, and confront the Machines. However, their real bodies remain inert, reliant on the sensory experiences of their physical forms to perceive themselves within the Matrix.

This unveiling of the Matrix-like nature of human existence suggests that we dwell in a realm where our consciousness is tethered to bodies, fashioned to emulate physical forms. However, this notion bears resemblance to Platonic ideals intertwined with Christian motifs. Socrates, Plato, and Augustine, all dualists, espoused the view of the immortal soul. Socrates posited that death is not the end of existence, it is merely separation of the soul from the body. Plato, on the other hand, contended that the intellect represents the divine aspect of the soul, which, upon death, transcends the inferior physical vessel to join the realm of Ideas or the spiritual domain of Forms.

However, my contention lies in the departure of the soul as a disembodied consciousness to heaven, a concept incongruent with apocalyptic literature and Judeo-Christian views of the eschaton. In Judeo-Christian theology, emphasis is placed on the resurrection of the body, as depicted in biblical narratives. Inquiries arise concerning the nature of our resurrected bodies when we delve into the culmination of end-time events, judgment, and the restoration of the heavenly kingdom on earth as these considerations hold significance within religious frameworks that anticipate a life beyond the present, offering a future imbued with hope and promise surpassing current experiences. Various religious traditions including Islam, Hinduism, Buddhism, and Sikhism, among others, harbor beliefs in an afterlife. For instance, jihadists willingly sacrifice their present lives for a blissful future with God, while Hindus endure present hardships in anticipation of ascending to a higher station in the cycle of reincarnation. Apocalypticism often emerges from societal moral decay, presenting visions of a better future as a catalyst for believers to draw closer to God by renouncing worldly desires.

The book of Daniel, regarded as an apocalyptic text, offers a narrative spanning ancient Near Eastern history from the sixth to the second centuries BCE. It presents a vivid depiction of judgment upon the dead, followed by the prospect of eternal life or punishment. Ultimately, it prophesies the dawn of a new age and the establishment of a new world order characterized by a new heaven and earth.

Christianity played a pivotal role in shaping Western beliefs regarding the afterlife, particularly emphasizing the resurrection of the dead with transformed bodies. This concept finds resonance in the writings of Paul, whose works exhibit traces of Platonic influence. It is essential to contextualize Paul's discussions within the intellectual milieu of his time, acknowledging his adept use of Hellenistic language to convey theological truths through philosophical concepts.

During Paul's era, Christians maintained a literal belief in the bodily resurrection, with Jesus's own resurrection serving as the cornerstone of this conviction. This belief was deeply rooted in Jewish literature and tradition.

The cities of Alexandria and Antioch emerged as primary centers for the development of Christian doctrine, where theological ideas were debated and refined within vibrant intellectual communities.

> Apostolic Christianity at first wanted nothing to do with the immortality of the soul. Christianity did not belong to that tiny, elite class of Jews who wanted to preserve their intellectual achievements after death; it would be at least a century, maybe two, before many Christians rose to the social level of a Philo or a Josephus. Christianity's beginnings were in the apocalyptic groups that believed in resurrection of the body. After all, the Jesus movement unexpectedly and tragically found itself faced with a martyred leader. It was natural, obvious in many ways, that a notion of resurrection would inform this group's continued narrative about its relationship to God; the surprise was that it believed Jesus to be already resurrected, which inevitably led both to the notion that he was divine and to the conclusion that the apocalyptic end-time had begun.[1] Philo of Alexandria thought that immortality was not an inherent quality of the soul, as the Greeks urged, but was a gift of God to a person who

---

1. Segal, *Life After Death*, 705.

would otherwise be lost in death. Christian theology of the afterlife was shaped by such Jewish perspectives.[2]

Plato's teachings undoubtedly had a significant impact on both Philo and Plutarch, who lived during the same period as Paul. There are compelling arguments suggesting that Paul, whether in agreement or disagreement, engaged with Plato's ideas regarding the soul or the existence of another world. Plato's philosophical framework provides the Greek foundation for the descriptions of inspiration found in the Greco-Roman writings of both Philo and Plutarch.

Moreover, examining the further development of Paul's eschatology through the perspectives of individuals who were closer in time to Paul offers valuable insights. These contemporaries of Paul provide a contextual lens through which we can better understand Paul's teachings and their evolution within the early Christian community.

> Origen claims that he is merely restating the Pauline concept of spiritual bodies. But he has traveled, in reality, a great distance from the apocalyptic mysticism of Paul. Origen's notion of a "spiritual body" has taken its lead from Paul but, like Valentinianism, the concept is the immortal soul of Platonism in disguise. He sees souls as the stuff of the stars and the perfected souls as the heavenly bodies. Origen allows everything but the natural immortality of the soul. For him, it is the saving work of God which immortalizes the soul, just as it was for Philo. This is certainly a possible and consistent way for Christianity to have moved. As it turned out, it was rejected. However, it was taken up by Gnosticism and later by Manichaeanism.[3]

References to Plato's teachings found in texts by Plutarch and Philo serve as historical evidence of the philosophical underpinnings present within Second Temple Judaism and early Christianity during Paul's time. These contemporaneous writings provide insight into the intellectual surroundings in which Jewish and Christian

---

2. Ellens, *Heaven, Hell, and the Afterlife*.
3. Segal, *Life After Death*, 573–74.

communities operated, indicating a foundation of philosophical thought that influenced their beliefs and practices.

Paul's eschatological teachings revolved around the resurrection of the body, which he envisioned as transitioning to a realm mediated by spatial dimensions beyond the constraints of time, space, and matter. This understanding is articulated within the confines of human language, which inherently imposes spatial boundaries. The place of mediation, where God reveals himself, is an eschatological event that exists outside the confines of temporality and within the realm of eternity.[4]

> Such works like Revelation and specific passages like 2 Corinthians 12:18 are often referred to as apocalyptic texts. Although scholars have been engaged in a perennial battle over what exactly defines "apocalyptic," many of them probe Jewish parallels to help them decipher passages where Paul delves into apocalyptic discussions, however defined. Jewish apocalypticism isn't the only parallel that illumines Paul's thinking. There are also similarities between these passages in Paul and two philosophical titans in the ancient world, Plato and Cicero. They crown their capital works with stories about a person raptured away to paradise who sees incredible visions and hears mystical messages.[5]

The revelation of apocalypse addresses the fundamental question: What fate awaits the wicked and the righteous upon death? Herein, eschatological salvation does not require an end-of-the-world scenario; instead, it may describe the way that apocalyptic literature gives hope to the righteous by looking beyond death (cf. 1 En. 22:1–14; 94:6—104:8[38]).[6]

It is worth noting that theologian Gregory Beale advocates for an expanded understanding of eschatology, suggesting that it encompasses more than just the culmination of history but begins

---

4. Evans, *Holy Spirit as Space*, 135.
5. Briones and Dodson, *Paul and the Giants*, 135.
6. Reynolds, *Jewish Apocalyptic Tradition*, 6.

with the transformative experience of being born again in Christ.[7] From this perspective, elements of eschatological imagery, such as the end-time temple, are viewed not only as future events but also as present realities existing within a different spatial dimension, made possible by Christ's redemptive work (as discussed in Heb 9:1—10:26). This eschatological beginning finds expression in apocalypticism, which encompasses the past, present, and future, unfolding in real time and urging exploration of the culture of humans and supra-creatures within the spiritual realm.[8]

John and the resurrected body embark upon a journey into a separate social dimension, detached from its physical shell yet intricately intertwined with it, reminiscent of the themes portrayed in the *Matrix*. In John's revelation, within various social spaces, the elements of the body materialize in dreams and visions, occasionally offering glimpses of the potential for the physical body to undergo transformation into a constantly evolving form parallel to that of Jesus's resurrected body. These manifestations occur within both temporal and eternal realms, highlighting the interconnectedness of the temporal and spiritual aspects of the self. Furthermore, in earlier writings, such as those based on Jeremiah, the image of humanity is illuminated by the presence of the Holy Spirit. Without the Holy Spirit, this image fades away. Just as God's form is revealed through the Spirit, so too is the human form. Throughout history, various forms of God have been revealed.

To explore this concept further, let's revisit the ancient Egyptian understanding of the soul. The Egyptians perceived death as a transition, believing that the *ka*, *akh*, and *ba* (soul) within each individual endured beyond the physical body's demise. According to their beliefs, after death, the soul embarked on a journey to the afterlife during the day, guided by Re, the sun god, only to return to its embalmed body within the tomb by nightfall. They envisioned Re sailing across the heavens on a daily voyage, while at night, he descended into the underworld, ferrying the souls of the

---

7. Beale, *New Testament Biblical Theology*, 235–36.
8. Evans, *Holy Spirit as Space*, 107–8.

departed.[9] Similarly, in Judaism, while there is an acknowledgment of various components of the human being, there isn't a depiction of these elements functioning independently from the whole being. In many respects, the Jewish conception of the afterlife shares similarities with the Egyptian narrative.

> Sheol beneath is stirred up
> to meet you when you come;
> it rouses the shades to greet you,
> all who were leaders of the earth;
> it raises from their thrones
> all who were kings of the nations.
> (Isa 14:9)

In Jewish apocalyptic literature within in the Hebrew Bible, Sheol is acknowledged as one of the designations for the realm of the dead. Referred to as "the pit" in certain verses (such as 15 and 19), Sheol is depicted as resembling the modern concept of hell, believed to be the destination for all the deceased. Most of the broad surveys on the conceptual history of hell have argued that the ideas of eternal judgment or future punishment of the dead do not emerge within ancient Judaism until the exile or the Hellenistic period. Implicit in this model is the idea that judgment and punishment of the dead were concepts borrowed from Persian and Greek culture, and thus represent a move toward the dualistic concept of the afterlife that is espoused by early Christians.[10]

The traditional hope in ancient Israel underwent a radical transformation with the introduction of the idea of resurrection to a glorious afterlife. This new hope became central to apocalyptic literature, featuring prominently in the Dead Sea Scrolls and playing a crucial role in the rise of Christianity. However, the transition in the nature of Jewish hope was not immediate or complete. Some Jews, such as the Sadducees, rejected the idea of resurrection. Nonetheless, early Christian literature offers further insights

---

9. Agai, "Resurrection Imageries."
10. Henning, "Weeping," 26–27.

into the realms beyond, emphasizing concepts such as *heaven* or *paradise*.

In apocalyptic visions and dreams, divine encounters or acts of divinity often unfold in realms beyond our worldly comprehension, existing within the eternal fabric of existence. Here, the conventional notions of past, present, and future dissolve into a unified tapestry of experience rather than a linear continuum of time.[11] Cullman's caveat, that eternity may be conceived as qualitatively different from time, is possible. In the eschatological drama of the New Testament, including the apocalypse of John, there is occurring time that has no boundaries or limits before creation or after the end of the world.

John's apocalyptic visions also present a dimension that transcends the confines of the material world, affirming immortality and placing humanity within a realm that surpasses the tangible. This investigation culminates in the assertion that God's self-revelation transpires through the agency of the Holy Spirit within a realm that exists beyond our immediate reality. Here, dreams and visions emerge as channels through which communication with the divine is facilitated. It is within this framework that we observe diverse transformations of bodily imagery.

The body exhibits the capacity to alter its form across different contexts. In Ezekiel, God appears in the form of a man crafted by fire, intending to purify the sinful and rebellious Israel, with his fiery wrath destroying what cannot be redeemed. These visions, imparted through fire, are bestowed upon Ezekiel as a divine gift.

In the book of Daniel, following three weeks, Jesus appears to Daniel beside the river Hiddekel, described as "a certain man clothed in linen, with a golden girdle around his waist; his body like beryl, his face like lightning, his eyes like fiery torches, his arms and legs like the gleam of burnished bronze, and the sound of his words like the roar of a multitude" (Dan 10:5–6). The fine linen symbolizes Jesus's purity, while Uphaz, potentially a renowned gold-bearing region, serves as the source of the fine gold for his girdle, symbolizing his righteousness. Despite Daniel's pursuit of

---

11. Cullman, *Christ and Time*, 10.

alternative means to reconcile with Israel, the Lord's judgment remains just and righteous.

Following Jesus's crucifixion, his appearances in his resurrected body reveal nuances shedding light on the nature of his resurrection. Initially, when Jesus encounters Mary shortly after rising, he instructs her, "Touch me not; for I am not yet ascended to my Father" (John 20:17). However, eight days later, he invites Thomas to touch him, saying, "Reach hither thy finger and behold my hands, and reach hither thy hand and thrust it into my side, and be not faithless, but believing" (John 20:27 KJV). The key difference in these encounters lies in Jesus's ascension to heaven, suggesting the transformation of his body into a resurrected form.

In Luke's account (Luke 24:39 KJV), during an initial postresurrection appearance, Jesus addresses his disciples' skepticism regarding his physical nature. They mistake him for a spirit, prompting Jesus to clarify, "For a spirit does not have flesh and bones as ye see me have." This statement unequivocally establishes the tangible reality of Jesus's resurrected body, distinct from that of a mere spirit.

These incidents underscore the uniqueness of Jesus's resurrected body, which retains physical characteristics like flesh and bones while transcending earthly limitations. The sequential revelations to Mary and Thomas, alongside Jesus's own explanation, affirm the corporeal nature of his resurrected form, dispelling any doubts or misconceptions regarding his identity.

READING REVELATION

As an initial point, the disclosure of Jesus encompasses celestial entities. In Karl Barth's seminal work, *Church Dogmatics*, while revelation is a component of his Christology, it serves to explain the book of Revelation. Within his systematic theology, he rejects commencing from a premise of historical understanding because he argues that man cannot discover God autonomously; rather, knowledge of God is attainable solely through God's self-disclosure in Christ. Exclaiming revelation as the exclusive fount of knowledge, Barth asserts that humans are welcomed into communion with Jesus Christ, entering a realm where God unveils himself and extends his presence to us. This marks a perspective from which Barth suggests a connection between eternity and time, which is pertinent to the culmination of temporal existence.

Barth's conception of time is fundamentally rooted in revelation, wherein God unveils himself. For Barth, Christology represents a divine act he characterizes as an event.[12] He contends, based on the event of Jesus Christ, that God allocates time for humanity. He articulates this as *revelation time*, emphasizing that the time God dedicates to us is marked by revelation. While Barth acknowledges God's creation of time, he distinguishes it from the time currently experienced, which he labels as *lost time*, a consequence of humanity's fall. He argues for the existence of a third time, a concealed time, stemming from God's protection of the tree of life in the garden. This time, originally intended for humanity, now remains hidden.[13] Barth suggests that our lost time and the hidden time once coexisted until the Christ event, where God manifested himself through the incarnation of Jesus Christ. The mediated revelation of Jesus Christ permeates temporal reality, establishing a dimension wherein humanity, existing within temporal confines, transcends into a third temporal dimension closely intertwined with eternal time—perhaps described as redeemed time by theologians. Barth unites God and humanity within this third-time dimension. In creation, humanity apprehends God's time; in lost time, humanity experiences its own temporal reality; and in the time of Jesus Christ, humanity encounters divine revelation. Barth effectively bridges the chasm between eternity and time, emphasizing that when God reveals himself through Christ, it signifies a moment of revelation—revelation time.[14]

Similarly, Jesus embodies both human and divine natures, bridging the realms of the eternal and the temporal. As the presence of Jesus signifies God's time for humanity, his revelation

---

12. Busch, *Karl Barth: His Life*, 47.
13. Busch, *Karl Barth: His Life*, 47.
14. Busch, *Karl Barth: His Life*, 45.

constitutes the true essence of time. Barth argues that two dimensions can coexist within the same space, implying a two-dimensional perspective on time. When Christ is present, temporal time is superseded, and eternal time infiltrates our temporal dimension. He delineates, "The fulfillment of time by revelation does not so far mean, of course, the completion, but it means only the announcement, the immediate imminence of the taking away of our time."[15] In Christ, the past and future converge, resulting in fulfilled time—the consummation of temporal existence.

For Barth, Jesus Christ represents a perpetual dialectical relationship, existing transcendentally in every moment and place. In him, eternity seamlessly intertwines with temporality, maintaining its eternal essence. Similarly, time assumes an eternal quality within him, without forfeiting its temporal nature. Through this perspective, Barth offers a resolutely Christian response to the conundrum of the relationship between eternity and time.[16]

In light of the relationship between time and eternity, the form of Jesus's body adapts to the spatial context in which it exists. Similarly, human existence within this lost time, during which Adam and Eve lived and experienced eternity, reflects this adaptability of bodily form. This notion prompts a closer examination of celestial beings as depicted in the revelation to John.

John's reference to the human body is similar to the body mentioned in the paradise of Genesis, prior to the fall. Adam and Eve were living in eternal time pretransgression and a temporal reality post-transgression. They were like angels who, when on earth with physical bodies periodically present themselves as humans on earth, but they differed in that angels are spirits without physical bodies.

Barth's doctrine concerning angels suggests that they are personal beings within the domain of God's kingdom, possessing a spirit nature distinct from God's. Described as "ministering spirits" in the book of Hebrews (1:14), angels, denoted by the term *pneumata* (plural form of *pneuma*, meaning "spirit"), share

15. Busch, *Karl Barth: His Life*, 67.
16. Cassidy, *God's Time for Us*, 12.

a similar nature to God.[17] Like humans, angels are creations of God endowed with intelligence, will, and affections (Luke 10:18). However, some angels have fallen from their original state and are no longer in communion with God (Jude 1:6). Acting as agents of divine Providence, angels provide revelation and contribute to the renewal of humanity as witnesses to God's word and actions.[18]

Rodman Williams suggests that the angels' function is intrinsically linked to God. They operate within God's presence or embark on missions assigned by him, lacking independent activity. Williams further emphasizes that angels are not mere impersonal forces or projections of human attributes but are indeed moral beings.[19] According to Williams, angels exhibit will and personality, distinguishing them from abstract forces and highlighting their role as conscious agents who serve God's purposes.

Throughout church history, angels have been recognized as ministering spirits, aiding humanity and serving as witnesses for God. Engaged in facilitating communication between God and humanity, angels manifest through various actions—appearing, speaking, and intervening—as they fulfill their roles in divine Providence.[20] Angels play many character roles in the book of Revelation, interacting with both Jesus and John.

In John's depiction of Jesus, he begins by positioning himself to describe Jesus's body in altered forms, which may seem esoteric and understandable only to those familiar with the context in which it is presented. This approach bears resemblance to the Kabbalah, an ancient Jewish tradition of mystical interpretation of the Bible, which distinguishes between "God as he is" and "God as he manifests himself on earth."

In the spiritual realm—which John indicates he is in by using the phrase "in the spirit"—where he encounters Jesus, he describes Jesus vividly: "Clothed with a long robe and with a golden sash across his chest. His head and his hair were white as white wool,

---

17. Williams, *Renewal Theology*, 173.
18. Williams, *Renewal Theology*, 188.
19. Williams, *Renewal Theology*, 177.
20. Williams, *Renewal Theology*, 172.

white as snow; his eyes were like a flame of fire, his feet were like burnished bronze, refined as in a furnace, and his voice was like the sound of many waters" (Rev 1:12–16). Here again, we see the unified body of Jesus being used to represent separate parts of a message to the seven churches in Asia. For example, to the church of Ephesus, he walks amongst the lampstands holding the stars, warning of removing the lampstand without repentance. To Smyrna, he is depicted as the first and the last, encouraging faithfulness until death. To Pergamum, he holds a two-edged sword, ready to wage war against false teachings. To Thyatira he presents himself as having eyes as a flame of fire and feet like burnished brass. His feet indicate that he has been through the fire and resisted the seductions of Jezebel. His eyes warn that he is able to search minds and hearts. To Sardis he holds the seven spirits of God and the seven stars. They have a name for being alive but are dead. Again, he is warning them to repent or he will come at night and catch them in their sin. The messages continue, each depiction carrying a specific message tailored to the church addressed.

As the narrative progresses, Jesus's body undergoes alterations in form with each change of scenery. In the fourth chapter of Revelation, John's spiritual location shifts, and he is called to ascend higher to receive increased revelation. He enters the throne room of God and witnesses the altered body of God, depicted as a large seal. Here, Jesus is portrayed as a Lamb standing as if slaughtered, taking the scroll from the right hand of the one seated on the throne. This imagery underscores Jesus's worthiness to open the seals that have been sealed by the Father who sits on the throne, emphasizing Jesus's sacrificial role as the Lamb who was slain.

Again, the cosmic bodies depicted in these apocalyptic visions provide contextual insight, suggesting continuity between earthly existence and the postresurrection kingdom. Relationships within the body of Christ are seen as enduring and essential to one's identity in the eternal realm. Thus, the interpersonal relationships forged within the body of Christ on earth persist in shaping the identity of believers in the postresurrection kingdom.

This underscores the significance of the human body as an integral aspect of human identity postresurrection.

Herein we see that the resurrected body is tangible and describable in the biblical resurrection scenes, and these depictions are not meant to use the body of Jesus for metaphors and symbols but as the actual body of Jesus altering its form in different spatial environments. The whole being is always present and serves as a constant reminder to the identity of Jesus. Whatever elements or composites we invent to represent the body, soul, spirit, or the human image as revealed prior to the formation of the physical body, neither can function independent of each other. In the postresurrection, the identity of a person remains the same. We must understand the body of Jesus in all its detail if we are to understand our own ascension to the afterlife.

OUT OF THE TOMBS

We recount that, during Jesus's resurrection, the earth shook, the rocks split, and the tombs were opened, with the saints' "total bodies" walking out and appearing to many in the cities (Matt 27:52–53). This resurrection bears similarities to 2 Baruch, who grappled with questions about the resurrection, asking, "In what shape will those live who live in Your day? Or how will the splendor of those who (are) after that time continue? Will they then resume this form of the present?" (2 Bar. 49). Baruch receives his answer, suggesting that the earth will restore the dead in the same form it received them. He continues, "For then it will be necessary to show the living that the dead have come to life again, and that those who had departed have returned (again). And it shall come to pass, when they have severally recognized those whom they now know, then judgment shall grow strong, and those things which before were spoken of shall come" (2 Bar. 50).

Some scholars, influenced by a more scientific perspective, raise questions about the physiology of the resurrected body. They expand the discussion within a metaphysical physicalist framework, which challenges traditional dualistic theories by proposing that humans are spirited bodies. According to this view, the mind and personality are inseparable from the physical form, suggesting a holistic understanding of human existence.

However, I propose a nuanced perspective that considers the physical body as foundational for the resurrected form, drawing evidence from instances in the Gospels where Jesus's postresurrection appearances transcend mere physicality. Instances in Luke and John depict Jesus appearing and disappearing suddenly when interacting with his disciples, suggesting a transformation beyond mere physicality—a transcendence of material constraints.

Additionally, I argue that our inherent spatial nature allows for God to alter our forms to suit different contexts, as illustrated in the book of Revelation. Jesus's metaphysical, spiritual, and physiological changes are necessary for functionality within the revelation-time context, indicating a dynamic relationship between our physical form and the spiritual realm, where adaptation and transformation are essential for fulfilling divine purposes.

Nancey Murphy, a prominent advocate of physicalism, contends that humans are spirited bodies, rejecting the notion of a separate soul. She challenges the idea of an immortal soul by proposing that spirited bodies are subject to resurrection.[21] While I align with Murphy's emphasis on bodily resurrection, our perspectives diverge on certain aspects.

Murphy references Keith Ward's argument regarding the criteria for personal identity in the afterlife, which includes memory, dispositions, habits, and practices.[22] While I acknowledge the importance of memory, I suggest that certain memories become inconsequential in the face of God's righteousness, as depicted in Revelation where martyrs awaiting vindication express no tension despite their past suffering (Rev 6:10–11). However, I agree with Murphy's assessment of Ward, emphasizing the transformation of memory to contextualize suffering and distress within a broader framework of learning and development, with joy relative to a

---

21. Murphy, *Bodies and Souls*, 68–69; Evans, *Holy Spirit as Space*, 79.
22. Ward, *Religion and Human Nature*, 304.

deeper consciousness of God's presence.²³ Physicalism offers valuable insights into the nature of the resurrected body; a nuanced understanding that integrates biblical narratives, theological perspectives, and philosophical insights is crucial for a comprehensive exploration of this complex theological topic.

Exploring the postresurrected body delves into the integration of body and soul across spiritual and physical dimensions, transcending narrow perspectives such as the purely mental realm often emphasized in scientific discourse. Philosophically, the double-aspect theory posits that the mental and physical are complementary perspectives on the same substance, eliminating the need for their separation.

Thomas Metzinger's physicalist view aligns with this notion, suggesting that the phenomenal-state space of a system exists within its physical-state space, emphasizing the importance of mixed spaces in understanding the human composite. Metzinger further argues against the existence of independent selves, instead conceptualizing selves as ongoing processes facilitating individuals' perception of unified entities, enabling integrated interaction with internal and external environments.²⁴ However, I disagree with Metzinger's reductionist perspective that denies the existence of independent selves. While his view provides a compelling explanation of how we experience a unified sense of self, it overlooks the spiritual and metaphysical dimensions of human identity. From a theological standpoint, the self is more than just a process or a byproduct of physical states; it is a unique, created being with intrinsic value and purpose.

Edmund Husserl's transcendental phenomenology offers another lens, emphasizing the suspension of presuppositions or biases to approach new experiences with fresh perspectives.²⁵ He introduces the concept of *bracketing* (epoché), suggesting that we can temporarily set aside preconceived notions to approach new experiences with a fresh perspective, unencumbered by biases that

---

23. Murphy, *Bodies and Souls*, 140.
24. Metzinger, *Being No One*, 22.
25. Husserl, *Idea of Phenomenology*, 10.

might hinder our understanding. However, scholars have raised concerns about the practicality of completely suspending biases or presuppositions. Critics argue that our present experiential horizon is deeply intertwined with our understanding and cannot be fully disregarded. Husserl's assumption that presuppositions can be suspended is valid, especially when we consider how differing spatial contexts can introduce us to new perspectives. James Dunn's interpretation of Pauline theology illustrates beings functioning within multiple dimensions, emphasizing our embodied existence within a social framework and our capacity for reflective thought and emotional experience.[26] This interconnectedness underscores the profound reality within and beyond the universe, shaping our sense of self across various contexts.

In addition to these debates, some scholars propose the idea that when the eternal enters temporality, temporality itself becomes eternal. But this concept does not resonate with the Johannine Gospel, which depicts Jesus as being born into the world, temporarily suspending his eternal existence to sacrifice himself for humanity. Thus, the ontological nature of the born-again believer involves a transformation from one state of existence to another, facilitated by the presence of the Spirit. The Spirit serves as both the internal presence of life and the external presence of God, enabling individuals to inhabit blended spaces without collapsing them into a singular dimension. Consequently, while Husserl's approach underscores the importance of suspending biases to understand phenomena, its application in the spiritual realm may necessitate meaningful consideration due to the unique dynamics at play. Both spaces may require a reduction in knowledge to facilitate a genuine experience in new spaces.

My own response is that the postresurrected body encompasses a holistic understanding of human existence, integrating body and soul across spiritual and physical dimensions. Jesus's resurrected body bears the scars of his crucifixion with equal significance to the relationships he cultivated with those who recognized him postresurrection. It is certain that all who follow Jesus into

---

26. Dunn, *Christology*.

the afterlife, those presently within the kingdom of God and living in the space constructed by the Holy Spirit for the born-again believer, will experience a bodily resurrection like his. Paul says, "If the Spirit of him who raised Jesus from the dead dwells in you, he who raised Christ from the dead will give life to your mortal bodies also through his Spirit that dwells in you. For the same Spirit that raised Jesus will also raise us and bring us into the presence of God" (Rom 8:11; 2 Cor 4:14). As we anticipate bodily resurrection similar to Jesus's, the diverse cultural and historical perspectives on the afterlife shed light on the varied spatial environments and perceptions of the resurrected body. This interdisciplinary exploration enriches our understanding of the complexities surrounding the postresurrected body and its significance across different contexts. The lingering question is: What will we be resurrected to?

CONCLUSION

In contemplating the intricacies of resurrection, we confront not only theological inquiries but also philosophical reflections on the nature of existence itself. Drawing from diverse religious traditions, philosophical perspectives, and literary narratives, we find ourselves immersed in a tapestry of ideas that challenge conventional understandings of life, death, and the afterlife.

From the biblical narratives of Daniel and Ezekiel to the philosophical musings of Plato and Augustine, and from the apocalyptic visions of John to the cinematic allegories of the *Matrix*, we encounter a spectrum of perspectives on the relationship between the body, the soul, and the divine. Each narrative, each philosophical discourse, contributes to our understanding of the human condition and our quest for transcendence.

We've grappled with questions of corporeality and spirituality, temporality and eternity, materiality and transcendence. We've contemplated the significance of resurrection not only as a theological doctrine but also as a metaphor for renewal, transformation, and liberation.

Presently, the concept of resurrection beckons us to transcend the limitations of our earthly existence and embrace the promise of new life, both in this world and the next.

The journey through Revelation, accompanied by the theological insights of Barth and the contextual understanding of celestial beings, illuminates profound truths about the interplay between eternity and time, the nature of divine revelation, and the enduring significance of interpersonal relationships within the body of Christ. Through the lens of Barth's Christological framework, we perceive time not as a linear progression but as a multidimensional reality, where the revelation of Jesus Christ serves as the fulcrum upon which the past, present, and future converge. Jesus, embodying both human and divine natures, serves as the bridge between the temporal and the eternal, offering glimpses of redeemed time within the confines of earthly existence.

The portrayal of celestial beings, particularly angels, within the book of Revelation underscores their role as messengers and ministers of divine Providence, serving to facilitate communication between God and humanity. Their presence serves as a reminder of the relationship between the heavenly realm and earthly affairs, as well as the enduring significance of moral agency within the cosmic narrative.

Furthermore, the evolving depictions of Jesus's body throughout Revelation signify deeper spiritual truths and carry specific messages tailored to the recipients, highlighting the intimate connection between spiritual vision and divine revelation. His sacrificial role as the Lamb who was slain underscores the redemptive narrative that permeates the apocalyptic imagery, emphasizing the transformative power of Christ's sacrifice in shaping the destiny of humanity.

The journey through Revelation invites us to contemplate the transcendent mysteries of God's plan for creation. It calls us to engage with these profound truths not merely as spectators but as active participants in the unfolding drama of salvation history, anchored in the hope of Christ's ultimate triumph and the establishment of his eternal kingdom. Through meticulous analysis of biblical narratives, we unearth truths about the nature of human existence in both earthly and eternal dimensions.

Central to this exploration is the tangible reality of the resurrected body, depicted vividly in biblical accounts as a palpable entity that transcends mere metaphor or symbolism. The postresurrection appearances of Jesus attest to the continuity of identity across temporal and spatial contexts, underscoring the significance of the physical form in understanding the afterlife.

Drawing from biblical texts and scholarly discourse, we grapple with questions surrounding the physiology of the resurrected body and the nuances of personal identity in the eschatological realm. While various perspectives, including physicalism and dualism, offer valuable insights, a nuanced understanding emerges that integrates both spiritual and physical dimensions of human existence.

Moreover, the interdisciplinary dialogue surrounding the postresurrected body expands our comprehension of spatial environments and perceptions of identity across diverse cultural and historical contexts. From theological reflections on bodily resurrection to philosophical inquiries into the nature of selfhood, each perspective contributes to a multifaceted exploration of the human condition beyond earthly confines.

Ultimately, as we await the fulfillment of bodily resurrection promised in Scripture, we are challenged to contemplate the profound implications of our identity in Christ and the transformative power of the Spirit dwelling within us as well as the Spirit we now abide within. In this anticipation, we find hope and assurance that our resurrected bodies will bear witness to the redemptive work of Christ, transcending earthly limitations to dwell in the eternal presence of God.

4

Locating Heaven

BELIEF IN AN AFTERLIFE has been a central tenet in many cultures and religions throughout history. These beliefs often vary greatly depending on cultural, religious, and philosophical contexts. The promises of the afterlife as conveyed in the perspectives of various groups, including Israelites, Jews, Hellenists, and gentiles, drawing upon relevant texts and literature from each tradition, suggests that the journey toward heaven is a critical piece to understanding the body's transition from earth to heaven.

In the Old Testament, the Israelites were promised an afterlife closely tied to their obedience to God's commandments. As aforementioned, the book of Daniel in the Hebrew Bible offers insights into Israelite beliefs about the afterlife. Daniel 12:2 states, "Multitudes who sleep in the dust of the earth will awake: some to everlasting life, others to shame and everlasting contempt." This suggests a belief in resurrection and a judgment where the righteous will be rewarded with eternal life, while the wicked will face eternal punishment.

Jewish beliefs about the afterlife evolved over time, influenced by various cultural and religious factors. In the Second Temple period, the idea of resurrection became more prominent in Jewish thought, as evidenced in texts like the book of Daniel. However, there was also a diversity of views within Judaism, with some emphasizing the immortality of the soul and others focusing on bodily resurrection. The Talmud, a central text in rabbinic Judaism, discusses the concept of *Olam Ha-Ba*, "the World to Come," where the righteous are rewarded with eternal life in the presence of God.

Hellenistic beliefs about the afterlife were influenced by Greek philosophy, particularly the ideas of Plato and Aristotle. The concept of an afterlife in Hellenistic thought was often associated with the soul's journey to the realm of the dead, such as the underworld ruled by Hades. In Homer's epic poems, particularly the *Odyssey* and the *Iliad*, the afterlife is depicted as a shadowy existence in the underworld where the dead reside. Previously, I alluded to Paul's use of philosophy and his influence on Hellenistic Jews concerning the afterlife. Paul, who was well versed in both Jewish and Hellenistic thought, skillfully incorporated elements of Greek philosophy into his teachings to resonate with a diverse audience. By engaging with philosophical concepts familiar to the Hellenistic Jews, he was able to bridge cultural and religious divides, presenting the Christian understanding of the afterlife in a way that was both accessible and compelling. His approach underscored the continuity and fulfillment of Jewish eschatological hopes through the lens of Christ's resurrection, offering a transformed perspective on life after death that contrasted with the more static and somber views of the Greek underworld.

The promises of the afterlife for gentiles varied greatly depending on their cultural and religious backgrounds. In ancient Mesopotamia, for example, the belief in an afterlife was often tied to the idea of a dark and dreary underworld ruled by deities. In Egyptian religion, the afterlife was intricately linked to the process of mummification and the journey of the soul through the underworld.

Herein we see that promises of the afterlife vary significantly across different cultural and religious traditions, reflecting diverse beliefs about the nature of existence beyond death. From the Israelites' expectation of resurrection and judgment to the Hellenists' vision of the soul's journey to the underworld, and from the gentiles' diverse conceptions of the afterlife to the evolving views within Judaism, these beliefs continue to shape the way individuals understand and navigate the mystery of life after death. Exploring these promises sheds light on how believers experience bodily resurrection and live out the promises of God in eternity.

PARADISE

Paradise and heaven are often talked about in the same biblical sense when in actuality they are quite different. The term paradise that originates from the Greek word *paradeisos* is from the Persian word *pairidaêza*, an enclosed space in reference to a garden or park. Its geographical location on earth was known as the garden of Eden (Gen 2:8-10). This paradise symbolizes God's original intention for creation—a realm of abundance, joy, and communion with the God. However, because of the fall of humanity and the eviction of Adam and Eve from the garden, paradise represents a realm of rest and bliss in the presence of God after the transition from death to life that begins with accepting Jesus as Savior. It signifies not only a physical place but also transcendence and reconciliation with God. In the New Testament, Jesus speaks of paradise in his conversation with the repentant thief on the cross (Luke 23:43). Some scholars suggest that "today" refers to the day Jesus returns. Nevertheless, I agree with those who believe that the thief would be in Christ's presence that very day. The kingdom is spatial and, therefore, an experience that is happening in the *now* moment.

In the Old Testament, references to heaven often emphasize God's sovereignty and transcendence (Isa 66:1), portraying it as the abode of angelic beings and the source of divine revelation. Heaven is frequently described as the dwelling place of God and the destination of the righteous. The term *heaven* encompasses various layers of meaning, reflecting both a celestial realm and a state of divine fulfillment. This vision of heaven transcends mere physical or geographical dimensions, emphasizing its spiritual and ethical significance. In the New Testament, Jesus speaks extensively about the kingdom of heaven, presenting it as both a present reality and a future hope (Matt 4:17).

In the Gospel of John, Jesus's statement, "I go to prepare a place for you," hinges on the preceding mention of "many dwelling places in my Father's house" (14:2). Some scholars draw parallels between Jesus's words and Jewish beliefs regarding Sheol. While Jewish tradition suggests that the departed embark on an afterlife journey, initially resembling a place of rest, there's ambiguity about the nature of this place. Is it solely a place of repose or a journey, echoing Aramaic interpretations? Nonetheless, it is now a place that Jesus entered to set the captive free and, from that moment forward, allow the resurrected to enter heaven.

In Isa 66:1, God poses rhetorical questions such as "What kind of house will you build for me?" (RSV) or "Where is the house?" (NIV). Rather than focusing solely on Israel's inability to construct such a dwelling, we shift our attention toward God, interpreting the question literally. The house built by God is understood spatially in its creation. It is no different than the kingdom of God introduced by Jesus. All who accept Jesus as Lord and Savior and repent of their sins, immediately enter the kingdom.

A starting point for our discussion on entering heaven could be recognizing that Jesus is indicating a place for his apostles to abide with him and the Father. When I earlier referred to a house as a spatial concept rather than a literal structure, I was highlighting Jesus's intent to create space in the presence of the Lord. Even if we interpret Jesus's words as indicating the preparation of a heavenly dwelling in the Father's realm, this interpretation seems at odds with the promise in Revelation of a new heaven and a new earth, upon which stands the new Jerusalem. These are not transient dwellings but enduring geographical realms that will exist postresurrection, aligning with the assurance of a renewed world. But their existence will be quite different from those structures in the material world.

John's vision in Revelation describes the arrival of the holy city, the new Jerusalem, descending from heaven onto a new heaven and a new earth, following the passing away of the old heaven, earth, and sea (Rev 21:1–2). He is writing to Jews who believe that their final resting place is on new earth. But the promise is different to the apostles. Taken against the Jewish background, "In my Father's house are many rooms. If it were not so, would I have told you that I go to prepare a place for you? And if I go and prepare a place for you, I will come again and will take you to myself, that where I am you may be also" (John 14:2–3 ESV) is probably to be understood as heaven, a spatial location where the Father gathers with those he promised.

The new Jerusalem is described as having a square base measuring fifteen hundred miles in length and width, with a height of at least fourteen hundred miles, forming a colossal cube (Rev 21:16). Despite its immense dimensions, it appears insufficient to accommodate an innumerable multitude of people. Hence, the notion arises that the new Jerusalem may serve a different purpose than mere residency. Rather, it could be conceived as a spatial construct designed for Jewish believers, to whom such promises were made. This spatial interpretation aligns with earlier scriptural themes, such as the human body being likened to a dwelling place for the various elements of the individual. Similarly, when Christians gather, they are portrayed as the temple of the Holy Spirit, and New Testament believers are often depicted as constituting the body of Christ, representing the church. In this context, the new Jerusalem can be viewed as a spatial construct of spiritual beings, with Jesus Christ serving as the cornerstone, and its structure grounded in agreed-upon beliefs derived from the teachings of the apostles.

The process of entering the afterlife has already commenced for those who have undergone spiritual rebirth, marking their transition into the realm of God's kingdom. As hinted previously, our identity and relationships within the Christian community have begun and endure even beyond apocalyptic events, as migrating communities traverse spatial dimensions. The biblical promises spanning from Genesis to Revelation paint a picture of a future realm where people from all nations, both earthly and heavenly, will dwell. While Judaism and Christianity are closely related, the promises to each religious tradition differ.

However, understanding the believer's location in heaven requires a holistic interpretation of Revelation's eschatological themes, recognizing the symbolic significance of its visions while remaining attentive to their theological implications. At the culmination of God's redemptive work, the heavenly realm serves as the eternal dwelling place where humanity finds its true identity and purpose in communion with God. By transcending human spatial limitations and embracing a multidimensional reality, Paul moves us forward in the discussion.

DIMENSIONS OF HEAVEN

Paul suggested the existence of three dimensions in our world, implying the presence of at least three heavens. While it might be intuitive to consider immediate atmospheric space as the first heaven, let us refrain from assumptions. First, it is important to establish that God's presence is on a spatial coordinate. Let us posit that a dimension requires at least three coordinates to acknowledge a common action or condition, and these coordinates must interact seamlessly. Two-dimensional maps, being imaginary, don't reflect reality, which is (at least) three dimensional.

Consider a sphere that transcends human space, inviting believers into a mixed space where the human and divine coexist, allowing God's presence and supernatural context to manifest. Similarly, the spatial dimension of heaven encompasses temporal reality, sometimes intersecting with it, creating a realm where the primordial essence of human beings is as much a part of the spiritual realm as it is of the earthly realm.

Moreover, our navigation through space in three dimensions—moving left or right, forward or backward, up or down—underscores the indication that the objects depicted by John in Revelation are also three dimensional. If we can agree that a dimension requires at least three coordinates to acknowledge a common action or condition, and these coordinates must interact seamlessly, then it is true, our atmosphere is the first heaven.

Additionally, everything around us, from the houses we live in to the objects we use daily, possesses three dimensions: height, length, and width. Because God's presence occupies a spatial coordinate, then he, too, enters our space as a being and not merely his presence. As the Letter to the Hebrews says, "But you have come to Mount Zion and to the city of the living God, the heavenly Jerusalem, and to innumerable angels in festive gathering, and to the assembly of the firstborn who are enrolled in heaven, and to God the judge of all, and to the spirits of the righteous made perfect" (Heb 12:22–23). This leads us to the book of Revelation.

John invites us into a realm where the human and divine coexist in intimate communion. This exploration underscores the profound theological implications of man's positioning in heaven and invites further contemplation on the nature of our celestial existence. In this divine-human interspace, we are called to reflect on the transformative power of spiritual union, where the boundaries between the earthly and the heavenly blur. Here, our understanding of salvation, grace, and eternal life is deepened, as we recognize our role not merely as passive recipients but as active participants in the divine narrative. This invitation compels us to reconsider our earthly journey, seeing it not as separate from but as integrally connected to our heavenly destiny. Through John's vision, we are encouraged to live with a heightened awareness of God's presence, allowing it to shape our actions, thoughts, and relationships, thus bringing the divine closer to our everyday experiences.

The book of Revelation has vivid imagery and many eschatological themes. Among the myriad of visions and symbols presented, the positioning of humanity within the celestial realm remains a subject of intrigue. This leads us to delve into the depiction of man's location in heaven as elucidated within the pages of Revelation, exploring the significance of this portrayal and its implications for Christian theology. Understanding man's location in heaven requires a careful examination of the text's symbolism and its broader theological context.

The throne room vision: Central to the depiction of man in heaven is the visionary experience of the apostle John as recorded in Rev 4 and 5. In this passage, John is transported into the heavenly throne room, where he beholds the majestic presence of God seated upon his throne. Surrounding the throne are twenty-four elders and four living creatures, each offering worship and adoration to the Lamb who was slain.

The significance of the twenty-four elders in discussions concerning humanity's place in heaven is particularly striking. These elders, commonly understood as symbolic representations of redeemed humanity, are described as adorned in white attire and adorned with golden crowns. Their proximity to the throne of God symbolizes their elevated status and close connection with him. To dismiss their presence in heaven as purely figurative or symbolic would overlook crucial aspects. While it is plausible that they possess symbolic meaning, their identity, proximity to the throne, and interaction with certain objects suggest deeper implications. They are closely linked with the promises made by God to them.

The marriage supper of the Lamb: Another key passage that sheds light on man's location in heaven is found in Rev 19:6–9, where the marriage supper of the Lamb is celebrated. In this eschatological banquet, the bride of Christ, symbolizing the redeemed community of believers, is united with the Lamb in a joyous celebration. The imagery of a wedding feast underscores the intimacy and fellowship enjoyed by the redeemed in heaven. As participants in this heavenly banquet, believers are granted a place of honor and communion with God. The portrayal of man's location in heaven as a guest at the marriage supper emphasizes the relational aspect of eternity and the fulfillment of God's covenant promises. Jesus discussed marriage suppers in two passages, Matt 22:1–14 and 25:1–13. In these passages, he refers to feasting in the kingdom of heaven, envisioning a gathering that includes individuals from various regions, symbolized by "many from the east and the west," as well as patriarchs such as Abraham, Isaac, and Jacob (Matt 8:11).

The new Jerusalem: Finally, Rev 21 and 22 provide a glimpse of the ultimate destiny of humanity in the new heaven and new earth. Described as the new Jerusalem, this celestial city serves as the dwelling place of God and his redeemed people. Its splendor and magnificence surpass all earthly conceptions, offering a vision of eternal communion and fellowship with God.

Within the new Jerusalem, believers are depicted as reigning with Christ. The absence of sorrow, pain, and death underscores the transformative nature of this heavenly existence, where humanity finds its ultimate fulfillment and purpose in communion with God. From the throne room vision to the marriage supper of the Lamb and the new Jerusalem, believers are portrayed as enjoying fellowship with God and participating in the unfolding of his divine plan.

At the core of the preceding discussion lies the recognition of God's relationship with believers, transcending mere social space to encompass their physical presence in coordinates that place bodily believers in heaven. This concept resonates with the Old Testament, where, before a physical house was constructed for God, his presence was symbolized by the sacred ark, essentially dwelling in a tent. It is important to note that this does not imply a literal depiction of God's body, but rather emphasizes God's presence among humans.

The progression of God's engagement with humanity evolves from the tent, where his sanctuary traveled with Israel, to the earthly temple and tabernacle housing his sacred presence, and finally to the New Testament references to heaven where no physical temple exists. Ultimately, John asserts in Rev 21:22 that, in heaven, the Lord God the Almighty and the Lamb are its temple, indicating a shift from physical structures to a spiritual understanding of God's presence.

In reality, when John speaks of houses, temples, and kingdoms, he is not referring to physical buildings but rather spatial constructs of the Holy Spirit, facilitating communion with God across various social spaces. Despite many scholars interpreting these dwellings in Revelation as figurative language, they hold a profound reality in another sense. Abraham, according to Heb 11:10, looked for a city with foundations, crafted by God, highlighting a spiritual longing for a heavenly dwelling. Christians seek the city that is to come (13:14) through the resurrection. How we envision our presence in heaven directly relates to our bodily existence in the afterlife.

NEW JERUSALEM

The journey of separating from the present earth in anticipation of a new one has been lengthy and tumultuous throughout history. Even in heaven, we bear responsibility for the journeys we undertake and the power we wield over earthly spaces. Abraham himself embarked on a journey to find the city, traversing various lands and negotiating boundaries, illustrating the intricate dynamics of power and identity among different nations. Historically entailed is the construction and justification of human dominion over others across diverse regions and epochs. In Rev 21:22–27 John says, "I saw no temple in the city, for its temple is the Lord God the Almighty and the Lamb. And the city has no need of sun or moon to shine on it, for the glory of God is its light, and its lamp is the Lamb. The nations will walk by its light, and the kings of the earth will bring their glory into it. Its gates will never be shut by day—and there will be no night there. People will bring into it the glory and the honor of the nations."

First, it is important to pause for a moment to focus on the light of the temple. Scholar David Aune's research leads to one of the best exegeses I have heard on this passage:

> There is some difficulty with the text as it stands, for the statement that the gates of the city will not close *by day* (ἡμέρας is an adverbial genitive of time) is true of all ancient cities. The text would be more comprehensible if ἡμέρας, "by day," were omitted, for then the text would read, "The gates of the city will never close, for there is no night there" (Weiss-Heitmüller, 4:314, bracket the term [ἡμέρας]). Charles solves the problem by substituting καὶ νυκτός, "and by night," for νὺξ γὰρ οὐκ ἔσται ἐκεῖ, "for there will [vol. 52c, p. 1173] be no night there" (2:173,

439 n. 5), which results in this translation: "The gates of the city will never close by day and by night." The import of the adverb ἐκεῖ, "there," may be that day and night alternate as usual *outside* the holy city, but within the city itself the light from God and the Lamb mean that there is no night.[1]

Herein, the prophecy in Isa 60:11–12 also references "your gates shall always be open; day and night they shall not be shut, so that nations shall bring you their wealth, with their kings led in procession. For the nation and kingdom that will not serve you shall perish; those nations shall be utterly laid waste."

In addition, during the judgment in John's revelation, the kings of the earth are judged and all those found to be unclean are destroyed along with the first heaven and earth (Rev 19:17–21).

Second, who, then, compose the kings and nations that approach the temple? The kings of the earth, whose names are recorded in the book of life, are still present according to Rev 21:24–25. In Rev 1:6 and 5:10, John identifies them as those who have been freed from sin by the blood through the sacrifice of Jesus, thus subject to his sovereignty. Here, we encounter the entrenched Jewish eschatological concept of nations converging upon Jerusalem in the eschaton, known as Zion eschatology, deeply rooted in apocalyptic tradition.[2] John echoes Jewish beliefs while simultaneously aligning his revelation of Jesus with Christian apocalyptic doctrine.

David Aune's theory stands out among scholars for drawing a precise analogy between entering into spatial domains such as kingdoms, cities, and temples. Although the phrase *enter in* is employed here to describe access to the new Jerusalem, it is evident that the city symbolizes salvation, blending the concepts of the people of God as a structure and the eschatological fulfillment of God's kingdom on a new earth. *Entering in* is therefore used here (and in 22:14) as a spatial metaphor equivalent to *entering into* the kingdom of God, a metaphor that occurs frequently in

---

1. Aune, *Revelation 17–22*, 1173.
2. Aune, *Revelation 17–22*, 1172.

the teaching of Jesus (Matt 5:20; 7:21; 18:3; 19:23–24; 23:13; Mark 9:47; John 3:5; Acts 14:22).³

The theme of the kings and nations of the world making an eschatological pilgrimage to see the light and glory of God in Jerusalem occurs several times in early Jewish literature (Pss. Sol. 17:31; Tob 13:11). The phrase *the kings of the earth* occurs eight times in Revelation (1:5; 6:15; 17:2, 18; 18:3, 9; 19:19; 21:24), and only in 1:5 and 21:24 are they not hostile to God and his people.⁴ In this discourse, it is important to point to the role of narratives spanning from Abraham to the end of the Second Temple period, encompassing processes of nation building. These narratives echo concerns regarding ethnic and cultural fulfillment of the kingdom. This discussion prompts us to contemplate our continued existence as complete beings, occupying the new world in a different context.

---

3. Aune, *Revelation 17–22*, 1174. See also Windisch, "Die Sprüche," esp. 171.

4. Aune, *Revelation 17–22*, 1171.

5

An Evolution of Ideas

LIKE MANY SCHOLARS, AUGUSTINE underwent a significant evolution of ideas and concepts as he aged. In his later years, he infused greater significance into his concept of the spiritual bodies promised to Christians, particularly by recognizing the continuation of human bodies in the afterlife, albeit in a modified form.

Augustine's reinterpretation of heavenly bodies suggested that human bodies would be resurrected as heavenly ones, resembling the body of Christ—flesh and bones, visible as on earth. This adjustment implied a transition from earthly bodies to celestial ones while retaining the essential substance of our present bodies. He articulated this in a sermon, expressing a newfound reverence for the flesh, once seen as an enemy, now embraced as a cherished companion in eternity.

Of paramount importance is Augustine's emphasis on the continuity of the human body, albeit in a transformed state. This aligns with New Testament Scriptures affirming activities like eating and drinking in the new heaven and earth, underscoring the continuity between the old and new realms. Augustine's reflections compel us to consider why terms like *heaven* and *earth* are employed to describe the new world if it does not bear resemblance to its predecessor, a question that echoes the language used in the book of Revelation by John.

THE POWER OF THE RESURRECTED BODY

In Luke's account, Jesus goes to great lengths to assure his disciples that he is not a disembodied spirit but a physical being. He invites them to see and touch his hands and feet, emphasizing the reality of his flesh and bones. He even eats a piece of broiled fish in their presence, further confirming his corporeal existence. This serves to dispel any doubts and fears they may have had regarding the nature of his resurrected body.[1]

Our perception of ourselves is often twofold, as we are not static but dynamic beings. The resurrection of Jesus presents a beacon of hope and reassurance, indicating that our transition into a new realm, guided by spiritual understanding, doesn't detract from our humanity but instead enriches and transcends it. It is an affirmation of the continuity of our identity, relationships, and experiences, while also pointing to the transformative power of the divine in our lives. The understanding of the body as a whole, as opposed to a fragmented concept, was prominent among early Hebrew Christians.[2] This revealed truth continues today, though limited to only a few tribes.

This "moral horizon provides a conceptual canvas on which Revelation's tacit and explicit moral themes and values are painted. It provides lenses through which we are invited to interpret moral reality and frame ethical discussion. It unfolds a moral context in which Revelation frames human existence, *being*, action, and moral responsibility."[3] In the book of Revelation the continued life is apparent based on the language used to describe the future existence of humans beyond death.

What is particularly significant is the affirmation of future human physical existence within the temple and now the new Jerusalem, evidenced by the glory and honor brought into the temple by the kings of the nations. As we continue this discussion further, David Aune offers an excellent critique on kings and nations entering new Jerusalem. He focuses on the scenario in Revelation where the destruction of the kings of the earth and their armies,

---

1. Evans, *Holy Spirit as Space*, 97.
2. Evans, *Holy Spirit as Space*, 102.
3. Lichtenwalter, "Tree of Life and Ethics," para. 3.

as well as the destruction of the first heaven and the first earth, are described. Yet, in Rev 21:24–27, nations and kings of the earth still exist (Rev 19:17–21; 20:7–9; and 21:1). He says,

> There are, however, similarities between the eschatological scenario in Rev 19:11–21:27 and *Sib. Or.* 3.657–731, which narrates the final events in four stages: (1) The kings of the peoples attack the temple in Jerusalem (3.657–68; cf. Rev 20:7–9a). (2) God defends Jerusalem and annihilates the attackers (3.669–701; cf. Rev 20:9b–10). (3) Zion is restored (3.702–9; cf. Rev 21:9–21). (4) The inhabitants of all the islands and cities will recognize the sovereignty of God (3.710–31; cf. Rev 21:24–25). Nevertheless, the ancient Jewish eschatological motif of nations coming to Jerusalem in the eschaton, i.e. "Zion eschatology," was so firmly fixed in apocalyptic tradition that it is necessarily included here.
>
> It is important to note that the LXX translator of Isaiah exhibits a theological agenda that included the inclusion of Gentiles in the people of God; cf. Isa 23:14–24:1; 62:4 (Roetzel, "Oikoumene," 163–82). In Rev 21:24–26, full participation in eschatological salvation is presupposed. This eschatological expectation was based in part on historical experience (Ps 68:29; 1 Kgs 10:23–25; Jos. *Ant.* 15.402; *J.W.* 5.187; 2 Macc 5:16).[4]

John's declaration that Jesus is given authority over every tribe, people, language, and nation suggests that what happens here on earth has major ramifications for living in heaven. Within the framework of Paul's conception of the born-again experience as articulated in Gal 6:15, the emphasis lies on the unity of believers in Christ transcending distinctions such as circumcision. This also echoes his earlier sentiment in Gal 3:28 and Rom 8:29, which emphasizes the obliteration of societal divisions like Jew and Greek, slave and free, and male and female, underlining the oneness of all believers in Christ.

Paul's intention here is clear: to discourage the prioritization of ethnicity, socioeconomic status, gender, or race, and instead

---

4. Aune, *Revelation 17–22*, 1172.

emphasize the autonomy of individuals, respecting their unique identities, cultures, and inclinations.

As such, I am convinced that Karl Barth's discussion of the concept of a tribal God as part of his critique of certain ways of understanding and speaking about God can be understood in multiple ways. Barth's use of the term *tribal God* is generally seen as a critique of a parochial or narrow understanding of God that confines God's nature and concerns to a specific group, nation, or culture, thus limiting God's universality and sovereignty. But God can be sovereign over the universe and kingdoms and nations and tribes without belonging to any one group over another. Although Barth's concept of a tribal God includes a critique of nationalism and parochialism, he is right in his critique of how nationalism can co-opt religious language to serve its ends. He argued that when God is portrayed as exclusively on the side of one nation or group, this diminishes God's universal nature and reduces God to a partisan deity. This tribal God becomes a projection of the group's own interests and desires rather than the transcendent God of all humanity. Barth emphasized that Jesus Christ's lordship is universal and not limited to any single tribe, nation, or people. He asserted that the message of the gospel and the sovereignty of God transcend all human boundaries and divisions. In his view, the God revealed in Jesus Christ is the God of all people, and any attempt to limit God to a particular group is a fundamental misunderstanding of the Christian faith.

Barth warned against the idolatry of creating a god in the image of one's own group or nation. He argued that this is a form of self-worship rather than true worship of the living God. He insisted that God's revelation in Christ is a critique of all human attempts to domesticate or control the divine. For Barth, belief in a tribal God has serious theological and ethical implications. Theologically, it distorts the nature of God and the message of the gospel. Ethically, it leads to exclusion, division, and often violence, as different groups claim divine endorsement for their particular agendas and conflicts.

AN EVOLUTION OF IDEAS

Barth's critique of the tribal God can be seen in the American context in which Christians have sought to reorient Christianity toward nationalism, racism, and other forms of exclusivism that seek to co-opt religious faith for narrow, self-serving purposes.

However, if we look at a similar concept of the kingdom of God on earth, we come away with a different view of God's heavenly intentions. Myles Monroe, in his book *Rediscovering the Kingdom*, says colonization is the process of transforming an extended territory to be just like the center of government from which it extended; that is, to manifest the nature and will of the ruler in the lifestyle, activities, actions, and culture of the territory.[5] The culture of the territory is the way of life for the citizens manifested in their language, dress, eating habits, values, morals, and sense of self-worth and self-concept.

Ultimately, colonization offers varied approaches to understanding coexistence in heaven. John's Revelation does not forecast a heaven marked by dominion over others across regions in the new world, a viewpoint we will explore further in light of judgment depicted in Revelation. In the new world, Jesus is king and Jerusalem's citizens are his servants.

In the *Journal of Theology for South Africa*, Simon Maimela elucidates liberation theology in the African context:

> God's atoning work in the life, death and resurrection of Jesus Christ is for liberation theology not a timeless, theoretical and a-political idea, an idea to be thought about and believed in, but rather what has happened to and with Christ constitutes a fundamental breakthrough for human life in the history of the world. For it now means that God has succeeded in breaking the power of sin and its consequences for human life both in this world and the life hereafter: It means that the face of the world has been turned up-side-down because a possibility of fellowship among humans is created, and because humans can create life-nourishing and humanizing structures.[6]

---

5. Monroe, *Rediscovering the Kingdom*, 26.
6. Maimela, "Atonement in the Context," 53.

It is these emerging structures aimed at humanizing society that we witness evolving within the kingdom now, and which will persist into the final kingdom. This conversion initiates a new reality where one perceives the world from within the kingdom of God, marking the commencement of a new history and narrative brought to earth through Christ. Undoubtedly, God has not changed his intentions for humans since creation, and he does not signal that we must abandon earth as the home of humanity, but declares that he will make a new heaven and earth.

As previously suggested, the idea of earthly rulers journeying to the new Jerusalem implies the participation of nations and their leaders, and it underscores the idea of the ultimate Jerusalem being established on earth in eschatological terms. For this scenario to unfold, the prophecy delivered by the angel regarding Jesus in Luke 1:32–34 must come to fruition. Mary was informed that Jesus would achieve greatness and be known as the Son of the Most High, and that the Lord God would grant him the throne of his ancestor David. He would reign over the house of Jacob forever, and his kingdom would have no end. When John mentions in Rev 21:24–27 that the kings of the earth and their subjects will bring the glory and honor of the nations, he is fulfilling the apocalyptic prophecy found in Daniel. John is making allusions to the Davidic kingdom and the monarchs of the Old Testament, specifically the kings of Israel, who would bring their splendor into the temple.

Daniel Boyarin suggests that the anticipation of the restoration of the Davidic king was intensifying in Israel during the second century BCE. He further elaborates,

> We find the prophet Daniel having a vision in which there are two divine figures, one who is depicted as an old man, an Ancient of Days, sitting on the throne. We have been told, however, that there is more than one throne there, and sure enough a second divine figure, in form "like a human being," is brought on the clouds of heaven and invested by the Ancient of Days in a ceremony very much like the passing of the torch from elder king to younger in ancient Near Eastern royal ceremonial and the passing of the torch from older gods to younger ones

> in their myths: "I saw in the vision of the night, and behold with the clouds of the Heaven there came one like a Son of Man and came to the Ancient of Days and stood before him and brought him close, and to him was given rulership and the glory and the kingdom, and all nations, peoples, and languages will worship him. His rulership is eternal which will not pass, and his kingship will not be destroyed." We can begin to see here a notion about redemption that is quite different from the expectation of the restoration of a Davidic king on the throne of Jerusalem. What this text projects is a second divine figure to whom will be given eternal dominion of the entire world, of a restored entire world in which this eternal king's guidance and rule will be in accord, completely and finally, with the will of the Ancient of Days as well.[7]

It is evident that God has meticulously laid out a plan for the new earth, one where his eternal reign and rule over his people are central. This plan fosters an ethical discourse wherein believers lead lives liberated from shame and guilt, embracing innocence and deriving joy from their relationship with the Lord.

In the culmination of John's apocalyptic vision, the final prophetic event unfolds. The kingdom of God encompasses the expanse of the new heaven and earth, with the new Jerusalem descending upon the earth, fulfilling the promise of the holy city remaining among God's people. The temple stands as the ultimate spiritual fulfillment of God's historical promises.

John envisions a new heaven and earth emerging as the former ones pass away, with no sea remaining. The holy city, the new Jerusalem, descends from heaven, and God declares it his dwelling among his people. This marks the beginning of a new era, characterized by the healing of the nations, the wiping away of all tears, and the eradication of death, crying, and pain (Rev 21:1–4). A river of the water of life flows from the throne through the city's streets, and on either side of the river stands the tree of life, bearing twelve kinds of fruit each month. Its leaves serve for the healing of the nations, and nothing accursed will be found there anymore.

---

7. Boyarin, *Jewish Gospels*, 39.

The throne of God and of the Lamb will be in the city, and his servants will worship him, seeing his face, with his name inscribed on their foreheads. There will be no more night, for the Lord God will illuminate everything, and his people will reign forever (Rev 22:1–5).

Herein we encounter three distinct spatial realms: the earth, the kingdom of God, and the city of Jerusalem within the kingdom, with the temple centered within new Jerusalem. As previously mentioned, the temple illuminates the city, but it is crucial to note that life extends beyond the city's confines.

This multi-layered spatial arrangement highlights the interconnectedness of different realms within God's plan. While the city serves as a focal point, representing the pinnacle of God's presence among his people, life persists beyond its boundaries, signifying the expansive reach of God's kingdom. Thus, while the temple illuminates the city, it also symbolizes the radiance of God's presence permeating even the furthest reaches of his creation.

Although it might initially seem like there is no continued life beyond new Jerusalem, the subsequent verse introduces promises for those who persevere and continue to do God's work until the end (2:26).

It is essential to understand that these promises are deeply rooted in the historical promises made by God, providing the necessary context for John's vision. Walter Casper adds,

> For the Jews of Jesus' time the Kingdom of God was the essence of the hope for the establishment of the ideal of a just ruler which was never fulfilled on earth. In that ancient Middle Eastern conception, justice did not consist primarily in impartial judgments, but in help and protection for the helpless, weak and poor. The coming of the Kingdom of God was expected to be the liberation from unjust rule and the establishment of the justice of God in the world. The Kingdom of God was the main element of the hope for salvation. And lastly its coming coincided with the establishment of the eschatological shalom, peace between nations, between individuals, within the individual and in the whole universe. Paul and John

therefore correctly interpreted Jesus' intention when they spoke, not of the Kingdom of God, but of his justice or of life. In other words, Jesus' message of the coming of the Kingdom of God must be seen in the context of mankind's search for peace, freedom, justice and life.[8]

We witness the emergence of a faith-driven community endeavoring to articulate a language and mission that resonates not only with its internal members but also with those beyond its immediate boundaries. This community envisions a novel societal framework wherein the ethical and spiritual teachings of Jesus transcend racial, cultural, and political divides. Within this evolving society, every individual is inherently a part of a diverse and equitable community, where believers find genuine liberation from oppression, poverty, and cultural marginalization. This envisioned civilization is harmonized with divine will, and the concept of the resurrected body becomes more comprehensible when considering the promises made by God to various groups prior to the ultimate realization of the new heaven and earth.

ANGELS

There has been contention over the starting point of angelology, whether it originates from ontology or if it is more closely linked with anthropology or Providence. Initially, angels were intertwined with anthropology, but Karl Barth delves into their role in Providence, highlighting God's gracious governance of his creation, attributing to angels the duty of tending to and nurturing all that God has made.[9] Barth tentatively entertains the notion of their existence as individuals (Matt 18:10; Rev 2, 3). He adopts Dionysius's teachings on angels, constructing a doctrine of Providence grounded in the biblical portrayal of angels as servants (Heb 12:22), messengers (Rev 4, 5), and witnesses within the framework

---

8. Kasper, *Jesus the Christ*, 61.
9. Lindsay, "Heavenly Witness to God," 7.

of salvation history.[10] He shifts his focus to their service to God, hinting at their ontological significance.

Wolfhart Pannenberg argued that Scripture does tell us something about the nature of angels, which the New Testament expressly calls spirits (*pneumata*) in Heb 1:4, 12:9, and Rev 1:4.[11] Further, he states, "We have to agree with Barth that emphasis is on service. Yet we should not on that account overlook or suppress the fact that they are defined as spirits. If we could not define their nature at all, then all that is said about their existence and functions would be indeterminate."[12]

Barth's dialectical disbelief in the nature of angels, which is an extreme attempt to disprove angels as personal spirits, paradoxically offers a sketch of the possibility of their existence as personal beings. While Barth may not delve deeply into the intricate principles concerning the nature of angels, his theological perspective on their function provides valuable insights into angels as ontological beings existing beyond the realm of the word.

Rodman Williams, a theologian associated with renewal movements, echoes Barth's views, suggesting that angels dwell within the realm of mystery: they appear and vanish, speak and disappear, act and seem elusive. They consistently appear intertwined with God's actions, existing alongside or in relation to him. The essence of angels garners minimal attention in biblical discourse; their activities, however, are of significant interest.

Like humans, angels are creatures created by God with intelligence that includes *will* and *affections* (Luke 10:18). Some angels have fallen from their first estate, no longer in fellowship with God (Jude 1:6). Angels are agents of God toward humanity in divine Providence that provide revelation, and are a part of the renewal of humanity as witnesses to God's word and actions. Rodman Williams suggests, as does Barth, that an angel's function is always in relation to God. In a real sense, they have no independent activity but are invariably portrayed as functioning in God's presence

---

10. Barth, *Doctrine*, 390.
11. Pannenberg, *Systematic Theology*, 103.
12. Pannenberg, *Systematic Theology*, 103.

AN EVOLUTION OF IDEAS

or on some mission from him.[13] But Williams goes even further, indicating that angels are personal beings and not merely impersonal forces that are either attributes of God, personifications of nature, or projected human beings. He insists that angels are moral beings.[14]

Thomas Aquinas referred to the Old Testament fallen angels using dreams to work divine trickery, as seen in the story of Saul and the witch of Endor (1 Sam 28:7). Fallen angels are known to exploit dreams for their purposes. Similarly, Jesus was shown visions by the devil during his time in the wilderness when he was led by the Spirit to be tempted (Matt 4:1–11). Throughout his ordeal, Jesus endures hunger, is taken up to a pinnacle of the temple in the holy city, and is ultimately shown all the kingdoms of the world. These visions or mirages in the wilderness are consistent with the fallen angels' use of visions and dreams.

Angels teach us how to interpret their visual language. Daniel said, "I came near to one of those who stood by, and asked him the truth of all this. So he told me, and made me know the interpretation of the things" (Dan 7:16). Gabriel assisted with the interpretation of Daniel's visions: "God said, 'Gabriel, make this man understand the vision'" (Dan 8:16). When angels mediated God's message, Daniel excelled in interpreting dreams and visions.

Although Barth maintains a distinction between angels within the context of mediatorial identification, he underscores their crucial ontological existence. This distinction sets a clear boundary between angels and humanity, designating angels as partners in an eschatological existence within God's kingdom on earth. As Wood suggests, angels "foreshadow the dramatics of human life as a kingdom of personal moral agents."[15] Since they, too, are free-will moral agents, their history informs our own. This provides another perspective on addressing the resurrected body by focusing on the ethics of the new earth, new Jerusalem, and the temple.

---

13. Williams, *Renewal Theology*, 188.
14. Williams, *Renewal Theology*, 177.
15. Wood, "Extraordinarily Acute Embarrassment," 330.

KINGDOM ETHICS

The ethical principles of the kingdom of God can be discerned from the teachings of Jesus, both past and present. In his Sermon on the Mount, Jesus praises the virtue of meekness, blessing the meek and assuring them that they will inherit the earth, symbolizing a shared ownership of the earth. He also promises that the kingdom of heaven will welcome the persecuted, drawing a conceptual distinction between heaven and earth. Both encompass the kingdom of God yet exist in distinct geographical realms.

Throughout different eras, promises of rewards have been extended to diverse social groups within ancient and modern communities, suggesting the potential for a renewed civilization across various geographical landscapes. According to these promises, one group might dwell in the temple, another outside the city of Jerusalem, and others on the new earth. The impact of these diverse locations on the resurrected body and the experience of continued life in the new world hinges on the construction of a world of promises.

In John's Revelation, Jesus offers various rewards to the churches:

- The church of Ephesus is promised permission to eat from the tree of life upon repentance (Rev 2:7).
- Smyrna is promised a crown of life (Rev 2:10).
- Pergamum will receive hidden manna and a white stone with a new name (Rev 2:17).
- Thyatira will have authority over nations (Rev 2:26–27).
- Sardis's members will have their names written in the book of life (Rev 3:5).
- Philadelphia's members will become pillars in God's temple (Rev 3:12).
- The Laodiceans will have a place beside Jesus on his throne (Rev 3:21).

These promises are not just future rewards but are intrinsically linked to the ethical and moral conduct expected of believers. They imply a continued existence for humanity where enjoying a fulfilled life are all rooted in a framework of ethical behavior and moral perseverance. Thus, Jesus's promises in Revelation incorporate a vision of an eschatological future where ethical living is both the means and the end, encouraging believers to embody these virtues in their present lives as a testament to their faith.

The concept of the kingdom of God and its ethical implications are central themes in Christian theology and practice. Ethics is the ability to recognize God's command in a specific time and place. Ethos refers to the practical decisions to be made in a time and place according to the recognition of God's commands.[16] This definition allows flexibility for interpreting and applying God's commands, acknowledging the dynamic nature of ethical decisions.

Rooted in the teachings of Jesus, kingdom ethics serve as a guiding framework for believers, shaping their attitudes, behaviors, and interactions with the world. Jesus's promises suggest a continuation of the foundational principles of ethics. Kingdom ethics begins now with the transformative experience of entering the kingdom by accepting Jesus, and continues into eternity. Its significance in contemporary society has transformative potential in individual and collective lives for future living. Central to these values are love, justice, mercy, compassion, humility, and forgiveness. Jesus exemplified these virtues through his teachings and challenged societal norms and power structures of his time.

Love stands as the cornerstone of kingdom ethics, encompassing love for God, neighbor, and self. Jesus elevated love to the highest commandment, emphasizing the love that God gives as imperative in the love God seeks for himself, neighbor, and oneself. This divine love is also a gift of the Holy Spirit, like all fruits. Human love does not compare to the love God seeks from his human creatures. God starts with the physical, social, and relational being, transforming it into something greater. Only God is capable

---

16. Barth, *Karl Barth Letters*, 10.

of showing love, justice, mercy, compassion, humility, and forgiveness as they are intended to be. God's ethic of love transcends boundaries of race, ethnicity, religion, and social status, fostering inclusivity, empathy, and solidarity.

Justice and mercy are inseparable components of kingdom ethics, calling for the pursuit of righteousness and the alleviation of suffering. Jesus denounced oppression, exploitation, and injustice, advocating for the marginalized, oppressed, and downtrodden. Jesus himself suffered as a sinner to allow the sinful to go free. Contrary to what some scholars might believe, the need for mercy underscores the importance of God's justice, challenging the notion that God does not punish the guilty. But God is a just God whose mercy indicates the intensity of his justice. Without justice as the polar opposite of mercy, mercy does not have the same force or emphasis.

Humility and forgiveness are transformative virtues in kingdom ethics, fostering reconciliation and restoration. Jesus modeled humility through his servanthood and kenosis (self-emptying love), inviting his followers to emulate his example. Forgiveness, as exemplified in Jesus's teachings and actions, liberates both the forgiver and the forgiven, allowing both to be transformed and filled with God's Spirit, thereby breaking the cycle of resentment and retaliation.

In contemporary society, marked by division, injustice, and violence, kingdom ethics offer a vision of a reconciled and flourishing community. Jesus's ethics critique the structures of oppression, inequality, and exploitation prevalent in society, advocating for systemic change rooted in love, justice, and mercy.

In the face of tribalism, kingdom ethics promote dialogue, understanding, and reconciliation across ideological divides. They challenge the culture of consumerism, individualism, and self-interest, inviting individuals and communities to prioritize the common good over narrow self-interest.

Moreover, kingdom ethics inspire activism and advocacy for social justice and human rights. They empower believers to stand in solidarity with the marginalized, oppressed, and vulnerable, amplifying their voices and addressing the root causes of injustice and inequality.

The transformative potential of kingdom-of-God ethics lies in their capacity to renew hearts, minds, and societies. By embodying the virtues of love, justice, mercy, humility, and forgiveness, individuals become agents of transformation in their spheres of influence.

Personal transformation occurs as individuals align their lives with the values of the kingdom. Societies are transformed as they embody the ethos of the kingdom, fostering mutual care and a shared purpose.

Furthermore, kingdom-of-God ethics envision a transformed world characterized by peace, justice, and flourishing for all creation. While the full realization of this vision awaits the eschatological consummation of God's kingdom, believers are called to participate in its realization here and now, bearing witness to its presence and power in their lives and communities. In doing so, they become agents of transformation, contributing to the realization of God's kingdom on earth as it is in heaven.

NEW EARTH

How do we live together? A comparison of the nineteenth-century Social Gospel, the twentieth-century Liberation Gospel, and twenty-first-century Progressive Pentecostalism reveals that each movement, at its inception, embraced an inaugurated eschatology within its kingdom-of-God theology. However, varying social contexts led each movement to develop distinct interpretations of an inaugurated eschatology that reflects God's coming kingdom.

Considering the Social Gospel, a kingdom-of-God theology that omits individual salvation as a fundamental aspect cannot be classified as a gospel but rather as a social order. The kingdom of God represents a community of believers on earth who adhere to kingdom principles while anticipating a future life with God. The message of Jesus constitutes an eschatological community already living in the new age he inaugurated. Similarly, justification is an eschatological event, bringing the final judgment's verdict into the present, making the church a community of hope that looks toward the future with confidence.

Personal salvation is inseparable from the social struggle for justice. Salvation is both social and personal, embedded in the theology of the kingdom of God. Although it has developed globally with varying theological views, movements like Women's Liberation and Black Liberation in North America interpret Scripture through the lenses of gender and race. While this is not the place to engage in a true hermeneutic of the Spirit that excludes the reader's horizon or an explanation of one's theological context, it is important to recognize the diversity in interpretation.

Some may argue that theology is future-oriented while acknowledging the *already* and *not yet*. Others envision a salvation inclusive of the poor and marginalized, believing that hope has already begun in Jesus, who went about doing good and healing the oppressed. His atoning work is seen as a historical breakthrough. Theology's fight for political and social justice ties salvation and reconciliation to caring for the poor, offering a comprehensive view of atonement.

However, these movements sometimes shift their focus to the collective, social aspects of human life and forget that love, justice, mercy, compassion, humility, and forgiveness start with Jesus as Lord and Savior. Without Jesus, an analysis of ethical life (*Sittlichkeit*), law, and morality within a community fails as a spiritual community—a community of believers transformed by the power of the Holy Spirit. Building communities in the afterlife will hinge on believers' stewardship on earth. One cannot be trusted with the riches of God without first proving he or she can be trusted.

SUMMARY CONCLUSION

Up to this point our journey through the chapters of this book has been a profound exploration of the intricate relationship between the spiritual and physical dimensions of human existence. Beginning with the introduction, "Making Flesh," we were reminded of

Jesus's dual nature and the unity of his body, setting the stage for a deeper inquiry into body concepts across history.

As we traversed subsequent chapters, we witnessed the evolution of these concepts from ancient times to the Middle Ages, marked by significant theological shifts, especially following the Nicene Creed's declaration of Jesus as both divine and human. This journey challenged traditional interpretations, offering a novel perspective on the body as a reflection of God's spatial existence, transcending literal understandings and cultural boundaries.

Delving into the mystery of the new body and its implications for human existence, we grappled with differing views on the nature of the resurrected body in the afterlife. Our exploration was enriched by reflections on the new Jerusalem, evolving ideas of the temple and new heaven and earth, reinterpretations of heavenly bodies, and theological discourse on angels.

Through it all, a central theme emerged: the interconnectedness of faith, society, and human existence. As we contemplated kingdom ethics and the promise of a renewed civilization, we were inspired to envision a future where humanity lives in harmony with God's will, embodying principles of justice, and compassion.

Ultimately, our journey leads us to embrace the kingdom now—a spatial construct of the Holy Spirit wherein we live, move, and have our being. Just as Paul declared to the Athenians, we recognize that God's presence is not confined to physical structures but permeates every aspect of our existence, inviting us to participate fully in the unfolding of a new kingdom on earth.

As we conclude this exploration, we are reminded of our identity as citizens of heaven and agents of transformation in the world. With hearts filled with hope and minds enlightened by deeper truths, we eagerly anticipate the fulfillment of God's promises and the dawn of a new creation, that significantly highlights the end and beginning of the spiritual quest on which we have embarked. That odyssey cannot be understood without explication of human existence within the spaces God has chosen to engage with us. Regardless of the location, encounters between God and humans suggests that there is something more to human existence that supersedes the physical realm. Whether on Mount Sinai, in the temples of Jerusalem, or in modern-day churches, the space where God encounters humanity brings an acute awareness of the fullness of our being. In some aspects of our physical existence, we are limited, but the threshold between the sacred and the profane serves as a boundary and a frontier that distinguishes and separates the two realms that does not limit us as spatial beings. In other words, we experience two worlds at the same time, enabling the passage from the profane to the sacred. In the New Testament, the quest of humanity is for the new being to regain access to the permanence of the sacred space in the Spirit through the work and role of Jesus and the Holy Spirit.

We must recognize that fully inhabiting a space requires commitment. While changing physical locations is relatively easy, altering the constructs of our spaces is far more challenging. Place refers to the physical locality of our bodies, whereas space encompasses the entirety of our being, including mental and social components. Mental space transcends physical limitations, yet for true presence in any given place, the various aspects of our being—mental, social, and physical—must converge. As we journey through our transformed existence, we will align ourselves with the spaces we consciously choose to inhabit.

Exploring the diverse beliefs about the afterlife across cultures and religions leads us on a journey into the depths of human spirituality. From the ancient Israelites' steadfast adherence to divine commandments to the evolving perspectives within Judaism and the Hellenistic influences on the soul's journey, each tradition offers a distinct perspective on existence beyond earthly bounds.

Whether it is the Israelites' anticipation of divine justice, the Jewish vision of the World to Come, or the Hellenistic portrayal of the afterlife's mysterious realms, these beliefs reflect humanity's timeless pursuit of understanding and transcendence. Amidst this diversity, common themes emerge—the yearning for spiritual fulfillment, the hope for redemption, and the quest for eternal communion with God.

AN EVOLUTION OF IDEAS

Across cultures and epochs, the afterlife remains an enigmatic realm that shapes individuals' perceptions of life's purpose and destiny. Whether it is through bodily resurrection, the immortality of the soul, or the journey of the spirit, the promises of the afterlife offer solace, inspiration, and a glimpse into the eternal mystery beyond mortal limitations.

Through dialogue, reflection, and mutual respect for diverse beliefs, we gain deeper insights into the human condition and the ultimate destiny that awaits us all. Paradise, as depicted in religious texts, symbolizes not just a physical locale but also spiritual fulfillment and reconciliation with God—a universal yearning transcending cultural and temporal boundaries.

Heaven, on the other hand, is portrayed as the supreme abode of God and the righteous, embodying layers of spiritual and ethical significance. From the Old Testament's emphasis on paradise to Jesus's teachings on the kingdom of heaven, both concepts resonates as divine sovereignty.

Symbolic imagery from John's Revelation to prophetic visions of a new heaven and earth illuminates humanity's place within the celestial realm, sparking theological inquiry. As we contemplate the throne room vision, the marriage supper of the Lamb, and the new Jerusalem, we glimpse the profound relationship between humanity and God.

The absence of literal structures in heaven underscores the transcendent nature of God's presence while highlighting the transformative power of divine communion. Ultimately, our understanding of heaven extends beyond spatial constructs to embrace a deeper recognition of our relational union with God—an enduring promise central to Christian theology.

In our quest to grasp the theological implications of the new Jerusalem, we encounter narratives rich in complexity, symbolism, and eschatological anticipation. From ancient journeys to contemporary theological discourse, the path toward the new Jerusalem is marked by historical realities and theological aspirations.

The imagery of the new Jerusalem, as depicted in Revelation and prophetic Scriptures, prompts us to ponder divine glory and human participation in God's redemptive plan. Through this exploration, I have aimed to contribute to a deeper comprehension of the complex interplay between physicality, spirituality, and the divine.

Paul's expansion upon the traditional Jewish concept of the body within the cultural context of Hellenistic Judaism sparked early interest among Jewish communities, but a shift occurred within the Judeo-Christian tradition upon encountering the transformative nature of humanity as portrayed in the Gospels.

Through a comparative analysis of Judaic, Greek, and rabbinic philosophies, this study has identified multiple aspects of *flesh* aligning with the concept of a unified physical entity, depicted as both spatial and resurrected on earth.

Jesus fashioned a body that is both spiritual and physical. This exploration of significant developments in concepts of the body throughout history has illuminated various perspectives on the human form.

Chapter by chapter, I have examined body rhetoric, properties, and the significance of the resurrected body on earth, challenging traditional interpretations and presenting alternative viewpoints. Ultimately, this research proposes a holistic understanding of the human body as part of a larger being, reflecting God's spatial existence and illuminating the mysteries surrounding Jesus's birth, death, and resurrection. The physical body holds a place in the afterlife that aligns with perspectives from the Hellenistic period, and it is crucial to recognize how the human form can alter its appearance when we are viewed as a spatial being.

Bibliography

Agai, J. M. "Resurrection Imageries: A Study of the Motives for Extravagant Burial Rituals in Ancient Egypt." *Verbum et Ecclesia* 36 (2015). http://dx.doi.org/10.4102/ve.v36i1.1457.

Aune, David E. *Revelation 17–22*. WBC 52c. Grand Rapids: Zondervan, 2017.

Avila, Wanda. "*The Diary of a Country Priest*: The Transcendent on Film." *Journal of Religion and Film* 10 (2006). https://doi.org/10.32873/uno.dc.jrf.10.02.01.

Barth, Karl. *The Doctrine of the Word of God*. Vol. 1, bk. 2 of *Church Dogmatics*. Edited by Geoffrey W. Bromiley and T. F. Torrance, translated by Harold Knight, et al. New York: T&T Clark International, 1936.

———. *Karl Barth Letters 1961–1968*. Edited by Jürgen Fangmeier and Hinrich Stoevesandt, translated by Geoffrey W. Bromiley. Grand Rapids: Eerdmans, 1981.

Beale, Gregory K. *A New Testament Biblical Theology: The Unfolding of the Old Testament in the New*. Grand Rapids: Baker Academic, 2011.

Bemporad, Jack. "Soul: Jewish Concept." Encyclopedia, 1987. https://www.encyclopedia.com/environment/encyclopedias-almanacs-transcripts-and-maps/soul-jewish-concept.

Boyarin, Daniel. *The Jewish Gospels: The Story of the Jewish Christ*. New York: New Press, 2012.

Bratcher, Robert G., and Eugene A. Nida. *A Handbook on the Gospel of Mark*. UBS Handbook Series. New York: United Bible Societies, 1993.

Bridge, James. "Homoousion." In *The Catholic Encyclopedia*. Vol. 7. New York: Appleton, 1910. http://www.newadvent.org/cathen/07449a.htm.

Briones, David E., and Joseph R. Dodson. *Paul and the Giants of Philosophy: Reading the Apostle in Greco-Roman Context*. Downers Grove, IL: IVP Academic, 2019.

Budge, E. A. Wallis. *The Egyptian Book of the Dead: The Complete Papyrus of Ani*. Clydesdale, 2021. Kindle.

BIBLIOGRAPHY

Busch, Eberhard. *Karl Barth: His Life from Letters and Autobiographical Texts.* Translated by John Bowden. Grand Rapids: Eerdmans, 1994.

Cassidy, James J. *God's Time for Us: Barth's Reconciliation of Eternity and Time in Jesus Christ.* Bellingham, WA: Lexham, 2016.

Collins, John J. *A Short Introduction to the Hebrew Bible.* 2nd ed. Minneapolis: Fortress, 2014. Kindle.

Cullman, Oscar. *Christ and Time: The Primitive Christian Conception of Time and History.* 3rd ed. Eugene, OR: Wipf and Stock, 2018.

Denzinger, Heinrich. *Compendium of Creeds, Definitions, and Declarations on Matters of Faith and Morals.* Edited by Peter Hünermann et al. 43rd ed. San Francisco: Ignatius, 2012.

Dew, James K., Jr., and Paul M. Gould. *Philosophy: A Christian Introduction.* Grand Rapids: Baker Academic, 2019.

Dunn, James D. G. *Christology in the Making: A New Testament Inquiry into the Origins of the Doctrine of the Incarnation.* Philadelphia: Westminster, 1980.

Ellens, Harold. J. *Heaven, Hell, and the Afterlife: Eternity in Judaism, Christianity, and Islam.* Santa Barbara: Praeger, 2013. ProQuest Ebook Central.

Evans, George C., Jr. *The Holy Spirit as Space for the Living.* Eugene, OR: Wipf & Stock, 2023.

Farris, Joshua R. "Souls and Bodies: Why We Still Matter?" *Didaktikos* (2018) 40–42. https://www.academia.edu/38076727/Souls_and_Bodies_Why_We_Still_Matter.

Fisher, Greg. *Rome, Persia, and Arabia: Shaping the Middle East from Pompey to Muhammad.* New York: Routledge, 2020.

Henning, Meghan R. "Hell." *Routledge Dictionary of Ancient Mediterranean Religions,* edited by Eric Orlin, 128. New York: Routledge, 2015. https://ecommons.udayton.edu/rel_fac_pub/128.

———. "Weeping and Gnashing of Teeth: The Pedagogical Function of Hell in Matthew and the Early Church." PhD, Emory University, 2013. https://etd.library.emory.edu/concern/etds/6m311p562?locale=en.

Husserl, Edmund. *Idea of Phenomenology.* Translated by William P. Alston and George Nakhnikian. Dordrecht, NL: Kluwer Academic, 2010.

James, George J. M. *Stolen Legacy.* General, 2023. Kindle.

Kasper, Walter. *Jesus the Christ.* New ed. London: Bloomsbury, 2011.

Kimmel, Paul. *Dimensions of Faith.* Eugene, OR: Wipf & Stock, 2018.

Kleinig, John W. *Wonderfully Made: A Protestant Theology of the Body.* Bellingham, WA: Lexham, 2021.

Lefkowitz, Mary. "The Myth of a 'Stolen Legacy.'" *Society* 31 (1994) 27–33. https://doi.org/10.1007/BF02693227.

Lichtenwalter, Larry L. "The Tree of Life and Ethics." *Perspective Digest* 26 (2021). https://www.perspectivedigest.org/archive/26-4/the-tree-of-life-and-ethics.

Lindsay. "The Heavenly Witness to God: Karl Barth's Doctrine of Angels." *SJT* 70 (2017) 1–18. https://doi.org/10.1017/S0036930616000442.

BIBLIOGRAPHY

Maier, Johann. *Jesus von Nazareth in der talmudischen Überlieferung.* Darmstadt: Wissenschaftliche Buchgesellschaft, 1978.

Maimela, Simon S. "The Atonement in the Context of Liberation Theology." *JTSA* 39 (1982) 45–54. https://onlinelibrary.wiley.com/doi/10.1111/j.1758-6631.1986.tb01479.x.

Martens, Peter W. "Embodiment, Heresy, and the Hellenization of Christianity: The Descent of the Soul in Plato and Origen." *HTR* 108 (2015) 594–620. https://doi.org/10.1017/S0017816015000401.

Martin, Ralph P. *2 Corinthians.* WBC 40. Waco: Word, 1986.

Mead, G. R. S. *Did Jesus Live 100 B.C.? An Enquiry into the Talmud Jesus Stories, the Toldoth Jeschu, and Some Curious Statements of Epiphanius, Being a Contribution to the Study of Christian Origins.* New Hyde Park, NY: University, 1968.

Metzinger, Thomas. *Being No One: The Self-Model Theory of Subjectivity.* Cambridge: MIT Press, 2003.

Monroe, Myles. *Rediscovering the Kingdom: Ancient Hope for Our 21st Century World.* New Kensington, PA: Whitaker House, 2004.

Moss, Candida. *Divine Bodies: Resurrecting Perfection in the New Testament and Early Christianity.* New Haven: Yale University Press, 2019.

Murphy, Nancey. *Bodies and Souls, or Spirited Bodies?* Current Issues in Theology 3. Cambridge: Cambridge University Press, 2006.

Norris, Richard A., ed. and trans. *Christological Controversy.* Sources of Early Christian Thought. Minneapolis: Fortress, 1980.

Omanson, Roger L., and John Ellington. *A Handbook on Paul's Second Letter to the Corinthians.* UBS Handbook Series. New York: United Bible Societies, 1993.

Pannenberg, Wolfhart. *Systematic Theology.* Vol. 1, translated by Geoffrey W. Bromiley. Grand Rapids: Eerdmans, 2010.

Plantinga, Alvin. *Materialism and Christian Belief.* Oxford: Clarendon, 2007.

Reynolds, Benjamin E. *The Jewish Apocalyptic Tradition and the Shaping of New Testament Thought.* Minneapolis: Fortress, 2020. Kindle.

Robinson, James M., ed. *The Future of Our Religious Past: Essays in Honour of Rudolf Bultmann.* Translated by Charles E. Carlston and Robert P. Scharlemann. London: SCM, 1971.

Schäfer, Peter. *The Jewish Jesus: How Judaism and Christianity Shaped Each Other.* Princeton: Princeton University Press, 2012.

Schaff, Philip. *The History of Creeds.* Vol. 1 of *The Creeds of Christendom.* Grand Rapids: Baker Books, 1983.

Segal, Alan. *Life After Death: A History of the Afterlife in Western Religion.* Crown, 2010. Kindle.

Sharp, Carolyn, ed. *The Oxford Handbook of the Prophets.* Oxford Handbooks. New York: Oxford University Press, 2016.

Sider, Ronald J. "St. Paul's Understanding of the Nature and Significance of the Resurrection in I Corinthians XV 1–19." *NovT* 19 (1977) 124–41. https://doi.org/10.2307/1560542.

BIBLIOGRAPHY

Siegal, Michal Bar-Asher. *Early Christian Monastic Literature and the Babylonian Talmud*. Cambridge: Cambridge University Press, 2013.

———. *Jewish-Christian Dialogues on Scripture in Late Antiquity: Heretic Narratives of the Babylonian Talmud*. Cambridge: Cambridge University Press, 2019.

Swinburne, Richard. "Soul, Nature and Immortality of the." The Routledge Encyclopedia of Philosophy, 1998. https://www.rep.routledge.com/articles/thematic/soul-nature-and-immortality-of-the/v-1.

Ulmer, Moshe. "A Brief Introduction to Rabbinic Literature." In *Righteous Giving to the Poor: "Tzedakah" ("Charity") in Classical Rabbinic Judaism: Including a Brief Introduction to Rabbinic Literature*, 1–44. Piscataway, NJ: Gorgias, 2014. https://doi.org/10.31826/9781463235970-003.

Ward, Keith. *Religion and Human Nature*. Oxford: Clarendon, 1998.

Wesley, John. "Sermon 54: On Eternity." Christian Classics Ethereal Library. https://ccel.org/ccel/wesley/sermons/sermons.vi.i.html?queryID=40236648&resultID=187166URL.

Williams, Rodman J. *Renewal Theology*. Grand Rapids: Zondervan, 2011.

Windisch, Hans. "Die Sprüche vom Eingehen in das Reich Gottes." *ZNW* 27 (1928) 163–92. https://doi.org/10.1515/zntw.1928.27.2.163.

Wood, Donald. "'An Extraordinarily Acute Embarrassment': The Doctrine of Angels in Barth's *Göttingen Dogmatics*." *SJT* 66 (2013) 319–37. https://doi.org/10.1017/S003693061300015X.

Wright, N. T. *Paul: A Biography*. New York: HarperOne, 2018.

Index

Abraham, 11–12, 78–79, 82
Adam, 13, 16, 61, 73
Agai, J. M., 57n9
Alexander the Great, 24–25
Aquinas, Thomas, 93
Aristotle, 23–24, 42, 72
Arius, 4
Augustine, 52, 68, 83
Aune, David, 80–81, 81nn1–2, 82nn3–4, 84, 85n4

Barth, Karl, 13, 13n19, 14, 14n20, 21, 28, 59–61, 69, 86–87, 91–92, 92n10, 93, 95n16
Baruch, 64
Beale, Gregory, 55, 56n7
Bemporad, Jack, 37n18
Boyarin, Daniel, 9, 9n14, 20, 24, 88, 89n7
Bratcher, Robert G., 45, 46n31
Bridge, James, 5n5
Briones, David E., 33n13, 34n14, 55n5
Budge, E. A. Wallis, 36n17, 43nn28–29
Bultmann, Rudolf, 28
Busch, Eberhard, 60nn12–14, 61n15

Casper, Walter, 90
Cassidy, James J., 61n16
Celsus, 2, 19

Cephas, 30
Charles, 80
Christ. *See* Jesus
Cicero, 55
Coleridge, Samuel, 1, 19
Collins, John J., 37nn19–20
Emperor Constantine, 4
Crenshaw, Kimberlé, 8, 20
Cullman, Oscar, 58, 58n11

Daniel, 58, 68, 93
David, 45, 88
Denzinger, Heinrich, 5n5, 6n7
Dew, James K., Jr., 24nn2–3
Dionysius, 91
Dodson, Joseph R., 33n13, 34n14, 55n5
Dunn, James D. G., 67, 67n26

Elijah, 37–38
Ellens, Harold J., 54n2
Ellington, John, 3n1
Enoch, 37
Er (valiant warrior), 33–34
Evans, George C., 14n21, 33n12, 40nn24–25, 43n30, 55n4, 56n8, 84nn1–2
Eve, 13, 16, 61, 73
Ezekiel, 58, 68

Farmer, William R., 28

INDEX

Farris, Joshua R., 12n17, 13n18
Fisher, Greg, 5n6

Gabriel, 93
Gould, Paul M., 24nn2-3
Gundry, Robert, 12

Hagar, 11
Henning, Meghan R., 38n21, 57n10
Homer, 36, 72
Husserl, Edmund, 66, 66n25, 67

Isaac, 10-11, 20, 78
Ishmael, 11

Jacob, 78, 88
James, George, 27, 27n9, 42, 42n27, 43
Jeremiah, 56
Jesus, 1-10, 12-21, 28-32, 34-35, 38-39, 41, 43-44, 46-48, 53, 56, 58-65, 67-70, 72-74, 78, 82-87, 91, 93-99, 101-2
Jezebel, 63
Joel, 25
John, 6, 35, 56, 58, 61-63, 65, 68, 74, 77-79, 81, 83, 85, 87-90, 94, 101
Joseph, 6
Josephus, 53

Käsemann, Ernst, 3, 4n2
Kasper, Walter, 91n8
Kleinig, John W., 18n24

Lefkowitz, Mary, 42, 42n26
Lichtenwalter, Larry L., 84n3
Lindsay, 91n9
Luke, 6, 59, 84

Maier, Johann, 7, 8n10
Maimela, Simon S., 87, 87n6
Martens, Peter W., 25n4
Martin, Ralph P., 4n3

Mary (mother of Jesus), 2, 4, 6, 13, 59, 88
Mead, George Robert Stow, 8, 8n11, 26n7
Metzinger, Thomas, 66, 66n24
Monroe, Myles, 87, 87n5
Moses, 26, 38
Murphy, Nancey, 12n16, 16, 16n22, 65, 65n21, 66n23

Neo (chosen one in the Matrix), 51
Nida, Eugene A., 45, 46n31
Niebuhr, Richard R., 29
Norris, Richard A., 7n8

Omanson, Roger L., 3n1
Origen, 2, 54

Pannenberg, Wolfhart, 29, 92, 92nn11-12
Panthera (Roman soldier), 2
Paul, 3, 10-12, 20, 23-24, 28-34, 36, 39-40, 43-45, 47-50, 53, 55, 68, 72, 76, 85, 90, 99, 102
Peter, 14, 25, 35
Philo of Alexandria, 23, 53-54
Plantinga, Alvin, 17n23
Plato, 23-24, 27, 33-35, 43-44, 52, 54-55, 68, 72
Plutarch, 23, 54
Pontius Pilate, 4
Praxeas, 7

Re (sun god), 56
Reynolds, Benjamin E., 34n15, 55n6
Robinson, James M., 4n2
Roetzel, 85

Sarah, 11, 20
Saul, 93
Schäfer, Peter, 8-9, 9n13, 20
Schaff, Philip, 4n4
Segal, Alan, 38, 38nn22-23, 53n1, 54n3

Sharp, Carolyn, 25n6
Sider, Ronald J., 28, 29n11
Siegal, Michal Bar-Asher, 7, 7n9, 8, 8n12, 11, 11n15, 12
Socrates, 23–24, 52
Stroumsa, Guy, 24
Swinburne, Richard, 28n10

Tertullian of Carthage, 7
Thomas, 59

Ulmer, Moshe, 26n8

Vilmar, A. F. C., 18, 18n24, 28

Ward, Keith, 65, 65n22
Weiss-Heitmüller, 80
Williams, Rodman, 62, 62nn17–20, 92–93, 93nn13–14
Windisch, Hans, 82n3
witch of Endor, 93
Wood, Donald, 93, 93n15
Wright, N. T., 23, 24n1, 35, 35n16

www.ingramcontent.com/pod-product-compliance
Lightning Source LLC
Chambersburg PA
CBHW050836160426
43192CB00010B/2046